Don't Call Me Rosie

The Women Who Welded the LSTs and the Men Who Sailed on Them

Kathleen Thomas

Thomas/Wright, Inc.
7190 S.W. Fir Loop
Tigard, OR 97223
www.thomaswright.com

First Edition

Library of Congress Control Number: 2004093014

Published in The United States of America

Published by:
Thomas/Wright, Inc.
7190 SW Fir Loop
Tigard, Oregon 97223
www.thomaswright.com

ISBN 0-9754854-0-7

Cover Design by Sacha Barkhuff

Front Cover: *LST 743*, Courtesy of: Lester Parker. Jul, Ann, and Vee Jurjevic on their way to work at Dravo, Neville Island shipyard.

This Book is Dedicated to my Mother, Ann Jurjevic Thomas; my Godmother, Vera Jurjevic Drab; and to my Aunt, Julia Jurjevic Kurtek.

Table of Contents

Introduction

Growing up in Pittsburgh, Pennsylvania, Kathleen Thomas would occasionally hear her mother Ann tell of her work, along with her sisters Vera and Jul, in the Pittsburgh shipyards during World War II. As our society grew more cognizant of the contributions and sacrifices by our citizens during WWII, Kathy became aware that women welders and their part in the war effort were rarely mentioned. She concluded that this was a story worth telling.

Kathy Thomas is the fourth of five children of Frank and Ann Thomas. Her family was an active part of the large Croatian community in Pittsburgh and she and her brothers and sisters were usually busy participating in local Tamburitza groups, i.e. Croatian folk music groups. Kathy could play a prim, a bass and an accordion, but unlike her siblings, her vocal skills were wanting.

Kathy found math and science to be more to her liking. After high school she attended the University of Pennsylvania and received degrees in geology and civil engineering. Upon graduation, she moved to Portland, Oregon and began her career as a civil engineer. Today she still lives in Portland and is president and majority owner of a consulting engineering firm, Thomas/Wright, Inc., in Tigard, Oregon.

On Kathy's journey from Pittsburgh to Portland, her life and attitudes have evolved. Like many young girls growing up in the '70s, Kathy was opposed to wearing shoes or going to war. Today she works closely with military personnel and serves as president of the Portland Post of the Society of American Military Engineers.

In researching this book, Kathy naturally started by interviewing her mother and aunts. This is the material for the first chapter - The

Jurjevic Sisters. The first chapter was easy. After that there were many weekends spent in dogged research and hard work. A request from her that was published in Reminisce Magazine resulted in letters from both women and men who had been involved in the war effort. The internet proved a real blessing. On it she could review shipyard publications, naval records, and newspapers. Whenever she found information on a woman welder, she would search telephone directories, trying to find the woman or one of her relatives. Surprisingly, her determination paid off and she was eventually able to interview many women that were welders. Some women were also able to direct her to friends that they had worked with in the shipyards. Eventually she had enough information to write about women welders at several of the large shipyards.

Research of the men that sailed on the Landing Ship, Tanks (LSTs) was relatively easy compared to the women welders. For one thing, subsequent marriage had not lead the men to change their names. The men are also well organized into an LST association that has regular reunions. Although the women welders sometimes attend reunions and other gatherings of the LST association, they don't seem to have their own organization. Many men were quite willing to contribute information for this book, either through interviews or through letters to Kathy. Their stories run the full gamut from light and humorous to serious and tragic. Many men described the rough seas that they encountered and expressed appreciation for how well the ships were welded. They all seemed to feel that LSTs are fine vessels.

All of the men and women interviewed for this book felt that they had made an important contribution to the war effort and are very proud to have served. Kathy agrees that they made an important contribution and they should be proud.

Robert Wright
April 2004

Abbreviations

DUKW	Descriptor for an amphibious transport vehicle. D=1942, U=Utility, K=Front Wheel Drive, W=Two Rear Driving Axles
HMS	His Majesty's Ship or Her Majesty's Ship depending on whether there is a king or queen at the head of the British government.
LCI	Landing Craft, Infantry
LCM	Landing Craft, Mechanized
LCT	Landing Craft, Tank
LCVP	Landing Craft, Vehicle, Personnel
LSM	Landing Ship, Medium
LST	Landing Ship, Tank
ME	Messerschmidt
PC	Submarine Chaser
PT	Torpedo Boat
USO	United Service Organizations

"No. We were not Rosie the Riveter. We welded ships. Rosie got all of the attention. No one even gave us a name."

- Ann Jurjevic Thomas

Chapter One

The Jurjevic Sisters

At Dodsi Bo Bo, a Croatian social club, they were referred to as the "Cool Cucumbers". At the age of 18, they would be old enough to weld LSTs but they had to be 21 to have an alcoholic drink. That was just fine with Vee, Jul, and Ann. They drank their pop and stacked the cans in front of them. The guys would buy them pop until their whole table was full.

"And then we would dance," Vee said, "Then all these old ladies would sit around and watch us dancing. And here we wind up to the same thing, the old ladies watching the young ones dance."[1]

There were six girls and three boys in the Jurjevic family. They grew up in a house that didn't have a bathroom until three of the Jurjevic sisters became welders and made enough money to share some of it with their parents so they could remodel the attic into bedrooms and add a bathroom.

Vera Jurjevic, or Vee, was the first one of the sisters to work as a welder at the Dravo Shipyards on Neville Island in Pittsburgh, Pennsylvania. The shipyard did not have enough men because the men were at war and it was hiring women, so Vee went. The pay was better than any other job she had before. Vee started in the east yard on May 1, 1943. She was 22 years old. Later, when Ann and Jul were working in the west yard, she transferred over to the west yard to be with them.

LST 1. Photo donated to U.S. Naval Historical Center by Captain Oscar C.B. Wev, USCG (Retired)

The Landing Ship, Tank (LST), more affectionately known as the "Large Slow Target" by the sailors who served on them, was built so that the ship could beach, discharge troops, vehicles, and equipment and then unbeach itself with the aid of anchors and winches. They were 328 feet long, 50 feet wide, and could carry a 2,100 ton load of tanks and vehicles.[2] They had a maximum speed of 10.8 knots. Winston Churchill wrote in his memoirs that the LST "figured so prominently in all our later operations, making perhaps the greatest single contribution to the solution of the stubborn problem of landing heavy vehicles over beaches."[3]

In the west yard, Vee worked in stainless steel on the gun fences. She says of the gun fences, "They were great big circles and you weld them together. Then they put them up and it was like a fence. The guns go inside of that. The ramps for the tanks had to be done in stainless steel. The stainless steel was hard work because it melted fast. The stainless steel was like oil."[4]

Lloyd Pace, a signalman on one of the LSTs, wrote about his LST's armament.

"Our main deck armament was so heavy and concentrated that very few Japanese planes would venture overhead. One 3" x 50" stern gun; twin 40 mm guns on each side of the stern; two 50 caliber machine guns on my communication open deck; two 40 mm guns in the bow; and four 20 mm guns on each starboard and port sides of the open main deck. When we were "at it", there wasn't much room for a plane. Each of our ships sent up the same barrage if Japanese planes ventured."[5]

Vee and the other welders had to wear heavy jackets and pants, even during the hot, humid summers. "And then you had to drag your toolbox," Vee explained, " it was all full of tools you had to drag with you. Then you had to pull the long hose from the weld machine."[6]

LST 1 was launched from Dravo's west yard at Neville Island on September 7, 1942. The Neville Island yards would produce 145 LSTs. Its last LST, *LST 1059*, was launched on April 14, 1945.

Vee rode with Frank McCann to work. Then Frank went into the service and gave Vee his car. She drove without a driver's license. "I never went to driver's school, I just got in the car and drove it. I was like those dumb 14 year olds that get into the car and they don't know what to do when they try to drive it. Well, that was me."[7]

One day she needed gasoline. And the gas station attendant asked Vee to back up. Vee could not back up because she did not know how. So she drove the car around the block and then pulled up to the pump where the attendant wanted her to go. Later, she knocked over her mother's fence in the front yard. She was confused about forward and reverse, put it into the wrong gear and knocked over the fence.

Vee, Ann, and Jul. Photo published in the Dravo Slant newspaper, November 6, 1944.

"There was a big fat red light and I stopped. The car went clich, clich, clich. And I thought baloney with this. So I quit driving it. I put it in the garage."[8] Frank later came home from the service and picked up his car.

In November 1944, the three sisters photo appeared in the Dravo Slant newspaper. The writer predicted that when their beaus returned from World War II, "It may be a triple wedding if the war ever ends."[9] The writer didn't know that in the Jurjevic family, it was considered bad luck to get married at the same time.

One day, while walking up Vincent Street with several friends and siblings, Vee heard Jack, one of her friends, say to her, "will you marry me." She pretended that she did not hear him.

For a time, Steve Drab lived next door and although Vee hates writing letters, she wrote Steve a few during the war. One day, Vee answered the door and there was Steve with a diamond ring.

Vee: "In October, around Christmas, or something, he comes up with a big diamond ring."

Ann: "You mean without your permission?"

Vee: "Yeah."

Kathy (the author): "So if you had not answered the door, it would have been another sister he married?"

Vee: "No, he'd come up and talk to my brother Albin."

Ann: "So you fell for the ring?'

Vee: "No, I didn't. He gave me the ring when he came home. He gave it to me real quick because he didn't want me to go with Jack."[10] Vee and Steve married on May 15, 1946.

* * * * *

On January 8, 1942, Dravo's Chairman, John Berg, and President, Vere Edwards met with Rear Admiral Samuel Robinson, Chief of the Bureau of Ships. The Navy wanted Dravo to build a number of LSTs with the marine engineering firm of Gibbs and Cox serving as a design agent. Dravo would become the "lead yard" for the follow-on design and engineering of the LST as more shipyards were brought into the program.[11] Rear Admiral Robinson told the two men at this meeting, "If these vessels are produced in the time required, the war will be one year shorter than it will be if we fail."[12]

On January 14, 1942, Dravo received a contract to be the lead yard for a 300 ship order. Sixty of the ships were to be constructed at Neville Island and the remainder were parceled out to the other inland yards.[13] These yards, which became known as the "cornfield shipyards," were located in Ambridge, Pennsylvania; Evansville, Indiana; Seneca, Illinois; and Jeffersonville, Indiana. Dravo had five of its first 60 LSTs built at its Wilmington, Delaware yard.

"Vee worked at Dravo and she thought I better go there too because the salary was good at that time," Ann explained. "We had to go to school to learn how to weld and how to adjust the machines for the heat. You couldn't adjust them too hot or it would melt. If it was too cold, it wouldn't weld."

By this time, Jul was eighteen, so Ann and Jul went to welding school together in the evening. They started at Dravo on July 17, 1943. On this day, Ann didn't know that 12 years later, her fourth child would be born and a place called Disneyland would open.

At first Ann and Jul rode street cars to work. They had to walk to Perrysville Avenue to catch a street car downtown and then catch another street car to Neville Island.

Then Ann and Jul met Fred and he drove them to work. "He found out that we were going to Dravo's," said Jul. " I don't even know where he lived. Did we ever pay him. No. Cheap. Cheap. Cheap."

Jul turned to Ann during the interview and asked Ann "Did he ever try and kiss you?"

Ann: "Yes, that's why I wouldn't go with him anymore."

Jul: "Fred was a good guy. He would bring mom cases of oranges. I guess mom paid him. He had a way where he could buy things. You couldn't get fruit then."

Kathy to Jul: "Did Fred try to kiss you?"

Jul: "Yeah, he tried to kiss me."

Kathy: "Both of you?"

Ann: "Uh, not at the same time."

Kathy: "Did you guys talk about it?"

Ann: "No. We were too embarrassed."

Jul: "I mean, he wasn't young, good looking. I mean he's an old married man."

Ann: "Old gray hair."

Jul: "He was probably 30 or 40. We thought he was an old man."[14]

Neither Ann nor Jul ever kissed Fred. Instead, they went back to taking the street cars to work.

After the British evacuation of Dunkirk in 1940, Winston Churchill wanted the type of ship which came to be known as the LST. Because the approach to the beaches was too shallow for ships to get near, troops were ferried by nearly 400 small boats from the beach to off-lying ships. [15] However, munitions and vehicles had to be left behind.

Churchill wrote in his memoirs: "The need arose for a larger, more seaworthy vessel which, besides transporting tanks and other vehicles on ocean voyages, could also land them over beaches like the L.C.T.

(Landing Craft, Tank). I gave directions for the design of such a vessel, which was first called an "Atlantic L.C.T.", but was soon renamed "Landing Ship Tank" (L.S.T.). The building of these were inevitably impinged on the resources of our hard-pressed shipyards. Thus, of the first designs, nicknamed by the Admiralty the "Winette", only three were built; others were ordered in the United States and Canada, but were superseded by a later design."[16]

Churchill requested that the British Chief of Staff send to the U.S. Bureau of Ships their concept of the LST. John C. Niedermair, Technical Director of Preliminary Ship Design, prepared a rough sketch. Niedermair changed the British's design of a 1/100 slope to a 1/50 slope, deciding this would be a better slope for a beach landing. With Niedermair's sketch and the aid of a group of British consultants, the Bureau of Ships developed the plans of the LST.[17]

After she completed welding school, Dravo assigned Ann to the west yard.

"I was doing vertical welding," Ann said. "Somebody tapped me on the shoulder. And I put my hood up and looked around. I said, well what do you want? He didn't say anything so I said, look, don't bother me. And I put my hood back on and I was going to start welding and he tapped me on the shoulder again. I said, what do you want? He said, 'well, do you know who I am?' And I said, no and I don't care who you are. And then he said, 'well, I'm your supervisor.' Well, I felt pretty little about that. But then he said that I was doing a good job on the welding."[18]

Because Ann was small, many times she was directed to weld in the tighter spaces of the ship, places where a larger person would not fit.

In early April of 1944, James Forrestal, secretary of the Navy, visited Neville Island and requested Dravo to deliver 15 LSTs by May

31. At the time, Dravo was producing six ships per month. The 15th ship, *LST 748*, slid down the ways on May 29, 1944.

"It was a real, real cold day," Ann said, "and I was welding. And I got cold. And they had a barrel there to warm yourself up if you got cold. I saw a lot of people going around the barrel to get warmed up. And I thought I better go and warm up, my hands were getting pretty cold. I came down and I stood around the barrel and the foreman on the job, he said to me, 'Get your ass up there.' I said, I'm cold. I have to warm up a little bit. He said, 'Get up there and weld.'

I got real angry with him because he didn't let me stand around and warm up a little bit. So I took all my gear and I went home. And then the next day, I came back to work. And everybody said to me, 'Why are you back? You are supposed to be suspended whenever you walk away from the job.' Well, I said, nobody said anything. I'm here to work. And the reason they didn't suspend me was because we needed 15 LSTs in a hurry. Roosevelt had put out an order and he wanted them done in a certain time. So I went back to work and nothing was said."[19]

It was at Javors, a Croatian Club, that Ann met her future husband, Frank Thomas, in 1941. Ann's mother and father and Frank's mother and father were immigrants from Croatia. Frank went to Javors that night to listen to a singing group, the Javors Singing Society. From the audience, he saw Ann and Vee singing with the group.

Later that night, Frank left Javors and about a half block away, he saw Ann and Vee walking to the street car stop. He pulled his car up alongside of them and asked if they wanted a ride. Vee opened the front door to get in and Frank told her that Ann was to ride in the front seat next to him.[20] As Frank once wrote, " I had my eye on her."[21]

"I didn't think much about it," Ann later explained, "It was hard for us to get home by street car and here was a ride home."[22]

On the way home, Ann asked Frank if he wanted to buy a ticket to their concert and dance. Frank said he would if Ann would let him pick her up to go to the concert.

On Saturday nights, Frank, Ann, Vee, Jul, and Frank's friend Joe, went dancing at Dodsi Bo Bo. Frank and Ann dated and planned to marry on June 12, 1942. On June 4, 1942, Frank got drafted and they decided to wait until the war was over to marry. [23]

Frank eventually ended up at Camp Kilmer in New Jersey. He had asked his father to sell his car so that he could use the money to buy Ann an engagement ring. When Frank received the money, he went to a jeweler near the camp on August 6, 1942. [24]

Frank talked the jeweler into selling the ring Frank liked for the money that he had with him. He had the ring mailed to Ann, thinking he would not see her until after the war. He wrote a letter to Ann the next day, telling her that he bought her a ring and that she should receive it by Saturday afternoon. He asked her to wear it and "someday when I get back you can let me put it on your finger the way that I should."[25]

But luck was with Frank. He got a 36 hour weekend pass and took a train to Pittsburgh on August 8th. He arrived at Ann's home to find the ring had been delivered that morning. So Ann gave Frank the ring and told him to put it on her finger. And so he did. [26]

Frank left the following day to return to Camp Kilmer. On August 11, 1942, Frank wrote the following to Ann:

"I'll never get used to being without you. There is a funny feeling in my heart, hoping for the day, that we can be together again. I am lonesome for you S.L.C., and always will be until I am back. You are always on my mind. It's tough, "Hon", and no one knows (even when I laugh) of what I am going through. But I'll come out in the end in good spirits, and come home to my love."[27]

The letter went on:

"I have the feeling that I will be one of those who do get through this war alright and come home. For now everything has been tough for me. The breaks haven't come my way. So when any thing starts bad it usually ends up well. That's why I feel that I'll have a silver lining at the end."[28]

Throughout his letters to Ann, Frank would call her "Hon" and S.L.C. Ann may have been called a "Cool Cucumber" at Dodsi Bo Bo but to Frank she was his "Sweet Little Cucumber."

On November 2, 1942, Frank sailed from Ellis Island to Casablanca. Not long after he arrived in Africa he received a small package from Ann. In it was a four leaf clover and a small bible. Ann found the clover and sent it to him as a charm. To this day, he carries it in his wallet.

Frank was in charge of the radio communications in his battery. In February 1943, he and his battery went to a small place outside of Algiers, called Mason Carriee. "One day," Frank wrote, " we had a weapons carrier truck and we went swimming in the sea out on the coast near Algiers. We got stuck in the sand as we were leaving and we had to push ourselves out. The sand was deep. But getting stuck in that sand saved our lives because after we got out of there, then just as we got up to Mason Carriee, the whole place went up in one big boom.

An ammunition train had been sabotaged and it blew up. The steel and shell and metal and everything else came down on us and we had to turn around and go back ... If we had not been stuck in the sand we would have been right in the middle of the blowout. So this was one of our lucky days in Algeria."[29]

Frank survived the war and he will tell you that Ann's charm and bible saved his life.

When the war in Europe was over, Frank was told that his unit would be going back to the States by way of Japan. "So, when we heard the bomb was dropped on Japan," Frank wrote, "and Truman had okayed the second one and Japan surrendered, we were so grateful to Harry Truman and for the A-bomb because we sure as heck didn't feel like going home by way of Japan."[30]

On September 25, 1945, Frank returned to Staten Island. He had been gone almost three years. When he got to Camp Kilmer, he called Ann and told her he was back safely. After he hung up, he found out that the Army was giving passes to New York for the weekend because they couldn't do anything with the soldiers until Monday. Frank got a pass but went to Pittsburgh instead of New York. He arrived at Ann's home around midnight and awakened everyone.[31]

He went back to Camp, then received a 10 day furlough, followed by a discharge. Ann and Frank married on Thanksgiving Day, November 22, 1945. Frank was tired of traveling, so they postponed the honeymoon for five years.

* * * * *

Dravo used an all-welded construction method of prefabricated sections and work-stagings. The traditional method at the time was for shipyards to build ships of riveted construction. Dravo used clusters of generators on skids to provide power for the arc welders moving around the site.[32]

In 1934, Dravo developed a transfer carriage. This device made it possible to move hulls progressively from the keel-laying position through a series of erection berths to the final position for launching. Dravo built 60 transfer carriages for use at the other inland yards.[33]

Jul recalls welding down in the "monkey hole" as the most difficult in the summer. Although she doesn't remember the exact part of the ship that they called the "monkey hole', she does remember how difficult it was getting through the small opening and going down the steel ladder with all the heavy equipment. With little or no ventilation, it was unbearable in the summer heat.

Jul started working with a fitter. "You tacked together, to hold it together. And if he got a bonus, you did too. So that was nice working with a fitter because you got a bonus. You earned extra money."[34]

Jul met Vic at a United Service Organizations dance. He was in the Navy and stationed in Coriapolis, near the shipyards. For about six months they wrote letters back and forth and then he came to visit and gave Jul an engagement ring.

"I did a bad thing," Jul says quietly. "While he was in the service, I returned the ring and I wrote him a "Dear John" letter. I felt bad because he was a real nice kid." Sixty years later, that "Dear John" letter still bothers Jul.

"I was scared, because he lived on Staten Island. It was too far away from me. He wanted me to come to Staten Island to meet his parents. I was afraid. I asked Mom if I could go. She said, oh no, you can't go. She wouldn't let me out of the house to travel like that by myself. I wouldn't even know how to get there. Then I thought, I don't think this is going to work."[35] Jul gave Vic back the engagement ring but she still has the Navy ring he gave her.

Ann, Josephine, Jul, and Mary at the Howdy Club, New York, June 11, 1944.

In June of 1944, Jul did make it to the Bronx, New York but she was with Ann and two girlfriends, Mary Holtje and Josephine Medved. They stayed with Josephine's sister and brother-in-law. Like typical tourists, they went ice skating, laid around the beach, saw the Rockettes at Radio City Hall, and went to Greenwich Village.

Josephine's sister and brother-in-law "lived in a big apartment building," Jul explained. "To get public transportation, you had to walk past this perfume factory. That stunk. You would think it would smell real nice, you know a perfume factory. But it stunk. It stunk like garbage."[36]

In 1944, Dravo sponsored a war bond drive in Pittsburgh and Allegheny County to raise funds for *LST 750*. *LST 750* was launched on May 30, 1944 before a crowd of 25,000.[37] Unfortunately, *LST 750* was sunk in her first combat action by a Kamikaze plane off Mindoro.

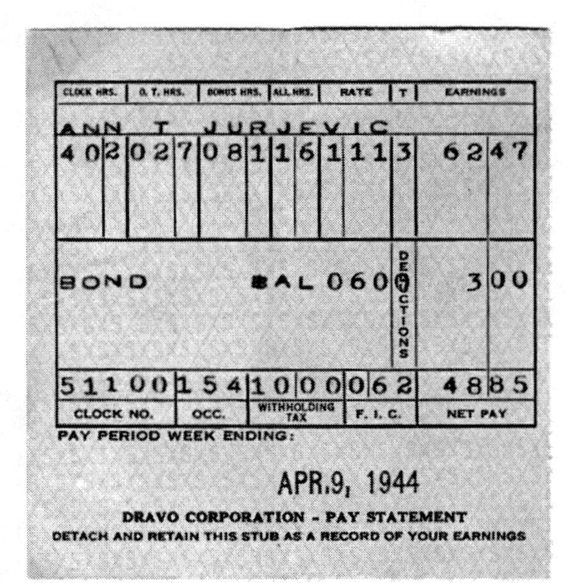

CLOCK HRS.	O. T. HRS.	BONUS HRS.	ALL. HRS.	RATE	T	EARNINGS
ANN T JURJEVIC						
40 2	02 7	08 1	1 6	1 11	3	62 47

BOND ■AL 0600 — DEDUCTIONS — 3 00

CLOCK NO.	OCC.	WITHHOLDING TAX	F. I. C.	NET PAY
51100	154	10 00	0 62	48 85

PAY PERIOD WEEK ENDING:

APR.9, 1944

DRAVO CORPORATION - PAY STATEMENT

DETACH AND RETAIN THIS STUB AS A RECORD OF YOUR EARNINGS

One of Ann's pay stubs. Note deduction for War Bonds.

Jul explained how she met Lou Kurtek.

"Vee was going out with Paul and Paul brought Lou to our house. I met him in the living room. So we went out. We went to a club. Lou went into the service. And I didn't write to him because he thought I was going out with George. I went to West View Park dance land. And Lou was there. And he asked me to dance. So I danced with him. And then he said he would like to take me home but he can't because he came out with this group of people.

Then he said - would I go to other dances. I told him we also went downtown to Arrogan Ballroom. Then in the meantime, another guy was at the dance. And he asked me to meet him at the Arrogan Ballroom. So now I had two dates. Then I thought, whoever meets me first and pays my way in, that's who I will go with. They were both there. I thought - oh, now what do I do. Then Lou hurried up and came over to me. And we went in, he paid my way in. So then I went with him.

We went together for about three, four months, something like that. We were at the Syria Mosque (a ballroom on the Northside). I was dancing with him. He said that he was going to get married. And I thought, oh you creep. You're going to get married and you're dancing with me. I said who are you going to marry? ' You.' That was my proposal.

We got engaged in November, I think he gave me a ring in November. We were suppose to get married the following June. But Vee had to have this baby and I was going to wait until Stevie was born. So then I got married in August instead."[38] Jul and Lou married on August 12, 1947.

* * * * *

At Dravo, the three sisters composed a song that they sang to the tune of the Notre Dame fight song.

We are the welders from Dravo.
We work in rain and even snow.
We are here to win this war.
We are so sorry that we can't do more.

We buy a war bond every pay.
An LST is on its way.
For our service men we pray.
Until they are safely home.

All three agreed that they hated when they had to redo other welder's work.

Vee: " You see they would come on Sunday. And they would do it real fast because they got a bonus. Next, when the inspector came the next day, they would all cut a little yellow mark."[39]

Ann, Vee, and Jul at the Pittsburgh Naval and Shipbuilding Memorial Bridge Renaming Ceremony, November 11, 2003.

The inspector marked the bad weld with a yellow crayon. Then a chipper came along and chipped out the old weld. Then better welders, like the Jurjevic sisters, would reweld the seam.

Ann Shearer's husband was a Chief Boatswain's mate in the Coast Guard Auxiliary during the war and served three years as a ferry command pilot. He piloted 84 LSTs down the Ohio River from Pittsburgh to New Orleans; Cairo, Illinois; or Louisville, Kentucky. The Navy pilots did not know the river so many River Boat Captains were used to ferry the ships down river.[40]

Les Parker served on *LST 743,* one of the 15 ships built at Dravo, Neville Island between April 1 and May 31, 1944. He invited the Jurjevic sisters to *LST 743's* reunion in Pittsburgh in the winter of 2000.

Mr. Parker wrote:

"Our first viewing of our new home for the next two years was on 12 May 1944. We wondered if such an awkward looking ship could really cross an ocean with a full load of tanks, troops, supplies, and equipment. It just looked too clumsy, with it's flat bottom and blunt nose. Of course we were seeing it on the ways, it had not yet been launched.

LST 743 was launched in a side ways launch on 14 May 1944, and to our surprise it rolled sideways north, back sideways south, bobbled a couple of times, righted itself and floated, proudly.

On our trip down the Ohio and Mississippi Rivers to New Orleans we collided with a barge loaded with someone's household goods, as they tried to cross our bow. Damage to the barge, total destruction, damage to the LST, scratched paint on the bow doors. All of the welds remained intact.

Our next encounter with potential disaster came in the Industrial Canal in the port of New Orleans, a very wide waterway at the entrance to the Gulf of Mexico. A communication problem between the pilot and our Quartermaster resulted in the LST colliding with a small ship, a pile of logs, and a wharf. Resultant damage, one crushed steel hull plate at compartment A405, requiring replacement of the steel plate. The welds held, intact.

In addition to our tank deck cargo, on our journey through the Caribbean, the Panama Canal and across the Pacific to the Admiralty Islands, we carried on a complete LCT (Landing Craft, Tank) on our weather deck, and 1/3 of an LCT chained to each side of the ship. In rough weather the strain on the hull of the LST was far beyond anything anticipated by the designers. Steel plates twisted, creaked, groaned and squealed, but the welds held fast.

LST 743 with a full load. Courtesy of: Lester Parker.

During the war, *LST 743* made over 100 beachhead landings, sometimes loaded with vehicles, tanks and personnel, sometimes with artillery pieces and ammunition, sometimes with hundreds of 55 gallon drums of gasoline and groceries, whatever the cargo, whatever the difficulty on beaching, the ship stood the test without any failure in the welds.

The supreme test came on October 9, 1945 off the coast of Okinawa. We had taken a Marine Detachment as occupation troops to Wakayama, Japan and were returning, empty, to pick up a load of supplies in the Philippines. Early in the morning storm warnings advised of an approaching typhoon, but indications were that it would miss us, so we continued on our way. Mid-morning the typhoon changed directions and headed straight for our path, moving at about 40 knots. With a top speed of 11 knots we were not likely to be able to avoid a direct hit.

In early afternoon, the winds had reached typhoon force (80 knots). The ship was being tossed about much like a jug with a cork in it. The flat bottom caused a terrific pounding as each 30 foot wave lifted the bow high, dropped it into a trough as the stern rose. As the bow dropped, then the stern dropped, steel deck plates rippled like cardboard.

Late in the afternoon of the 9th our wind gauge broke as winds hit 120 knots, seas were running 40 feet, the ship was taking a pounding that was far in excess of anything ever anticipated. We were now getting the up and down motion mixed with a twisting motion causing the ship to shudder with every wave. No one was allowed on deck, and all gear was double lashed. Then suddenly, dead silence, no wind almost calm seas. We had hit the eye.

Within an hour we were again buffeted, pitched, tossed and rolled in all directions as the backside of the typhoon hit the ship. We now had a major leak around the bow doors where the rubber seals had been twisted out of shape.

Finally the storm passed over the ship, blessed relief after hours of near terror. A full inspection by damage control revealed that no welded seams had been damaged, the hull was intact, the crew was safe.

Thank you Dravo Lady Welders. You saved our lives."[41]

Chapter Two

Just Another Day in the Shipyard

It was Christmas Eve 1942 when Dravo, at Neville Island, accepted women into its welding school for the first time. The first women welders went to work in the west yard. The February 26, 1943 issue of the *Dravo Slant* reported:

"A day to be remembered is December 24. It was on that day ... that the bars were let down - the bars forbidding women from the stalls of the Welding School. Progress was on the march as women, a full baker's dozen of them, took their places with hood and torch. Young and attractive, they were here to do a man's work. Imbued with a desire to play their part in a scheme so vague and vast, so incomprehensible, that even welding - a man's art - seemed mild and inviting."[1]

At the end of the article, Training Director Michael Evancho is quoted as saying, "Women will succeed in welding because of their innate dexterity, patience, and rapid adaptability."[2]

Johanna Aul doesn't recall how she heard about the welding jobs at Dravo but she knew one of the welding instructors, Boles Dawgiello. Johanna had two children who were going to school. Her husband was working as an electrician at Jones & Laughlin Steel Corporation. They worked different shifts and Johanna's mother helped with the children.

Johanna enjoyed the welding. When asked if she recalls any particular experience, she replied "We went about our business. Nothing exciting."[3]

Johanna worked for about a year and quit when she became pregnant with her third child.

Winston Churchill was concerned that proceeding with "Overlord", the invasion of Normandy, in May would remove LSTs from the Italy invasions. In his book, *Closing the Ring* and in the section, "Deadlock on the Third Front", he writes:

"In this period of the war all the great strategic combinations of the Western Powers were restricted and distorted by the shortage of tank landing-craft for the transport, not so much of tanks, but of vehicles of all kinds. The letters "L.S.T." (Landing Ship, Tanks) are burnt upon the minds of all those who dealt with military affairs in this period. We had invaded Italy in strong force. We had an army there which, if not supported, might be entirely cast away, giving Hitler the greatest triumph he had had since the fall of France. On the other hand, there could be no question of our not making the "Overlord" attack in 1944. The utmost I asked for was an easement, if necessary, of two months - i.e. from some time in May 1944 to some time in July.

This would meet the problem of the landing-craft. Instead of their having to return to England in the late autumn of 1943 before the winter gales, they could go in the early spring of 1944. If however the May date were insisted upon pedantically, and interpreted as May 1, the peril to the Allied Army in Italy seemed beyond remedy ... There were masses of troops standing idle in Africa ... The one thing that stood between these and effective operation in Italy was the L.S.T.s and the main thing that stood between us and the L.S.T.s was the insistence upon an early date for their return to Britain."[4]

Marie Slavonic was living with her brother and sister-in-law. Marie's parents had passed away. "Everybody was getting hired down there (Dravo shipyard) at the time. They kept saying, go down, go down, and apply. You'll get on. So that's what I did. Just went down there and applied and that's how I got to work there."[5]

Marie took the streetcar to work. She did all three types (vertical, horizontal, and overhead) of welding. She will tell you, "Nothing exciting happened. All we did was go to work, weld, and go home. Then go the next day. Go to work. Same thing. Same routine."[6]

Marie would have continued welding after the war if Dravo hadn't laid her off. She remembers that some of the women went to Delaware (Dravo's shipyard in Wilmington) after they got their notice. "This one girl, she wanted me to go with her but my brother and sister-in-law wouldn't let me go. They said no because it will close down and you'll be back home."[7]

One of the women Marie worked with asked Marie to be a bridesmaid in her wedding. One of the ushers was Joe Talpas, a Merchant Marine home on leave. Marie and Joe later married.

* * * * *

In a telegram dated April 16, 1944 to General George Marshall, Churchill expressed his strong support for maintaining the thrust in Italy and his frustration about the shortage of landing craft. His fifth and final point read in part:

"The whole of this difficult question only arises out of the absurd shortage of the L.S.T.s. How is it that the plans of two great empires like Britain and the United States should be so much hamstrung and limited by a hundred or two of these particular vessels will never be understood by history."[8]

Ann Grindel was the fourth oldest of 12 children. She was 19 years old and living at home in Mt. Troy, working downtown when she heard that Dravo was looking for welders. In 1943, she would walk about a mile to catch the streetcar downtown and then catch a second streetcar to Neville Island. It would take almost two hours to get there.

She worked the second shift in the west yard and she wouldn't return home until after 2:00 AM.

After Ann had been with Dravo for awhile, she met people who drove. After work, she and a male coworker would get a ride to Ravine Street. "It's a big steep hill that goes down to East Ohio Street. This fellow, he lived on Troy Hill and I lived on Mt. Troy. We would walk up those steps, this big steep hill, and he would walk me up to Mt. Troy and then go back down to his house. Which I thought was great."[9]

Occasionally, Ann and her friends would go to the night club on Neville Island after work. But it wasn't too often because you had to find someone to drive you home.

Ann knew a young man, Don, who would dance with her and her friends at the church on Troy Hill. One day Don stopped by with his friend, Bob Toia, and introduced Bob to her. "I was going with somebody else and this other fellow was leaving and Bob was the one that took us to the station for him (Ann's boyfriend) to take off for the Navy."[10]

Shortly after that, Bob went into the Air Force. He and Ann corresponded throughout the war and when he came home on leave, they became engaged. Ann Grindel and Bob Toia married on February 28, 1946.

When asked about being a welder on the LSTs at Dravo, Ann will tell you:

"I thought it was the greatest job I ever had. Although I got a lot of arc welds. My eyes. I couldn't see. But that happens almost to everybody. You got a flash from the welding. It blinded you for awhile. You had a sore eye for awhile. But it always healed up.

It was really rewarding and I was glad I did it. Even today when I see some of the old things on television, I think - Boy, that's what I did! Some of those kids were on some of those boats that came out of Pittsburgh."[11]

Ed Neubauer was one of those kids on one those boats that came out of Pittsburgh. He was 18 and a signalman on *LST 48*. Ed recalls:

"One dramatic experience was when we left the United States. We went up to Halifax, Nova Scotia. We went into a convoy to go to England. Which was in February. It was very, very bad weather in the North Atlantic, which is typical. We ended up with a 10 foot crack across the deck and side of the ship, right amidships. We carried six boats and broke two of those up. But we made it."[12]

LST 48 was repaired in England and went on to participate in the invasion on Normandy and went into Utah Beach.

"For a bunch of kids, it was pretty scary. We didn't know what was going to happen. We had to wear gas impregnating clothing and have a gas mask, just in case. Which never happened, fortunately. Lots of fire works.

We were suppose to unload quickly and then convert to a hospital ship to take the wounded back to England. Well, it didn't happen because of bad weather. We sat there with a bunch of cargo, trucks and tanks and stuff on board. And wounded coming aboard. The surgeons working on them on the mess tables. Which were set up to do that. Instead of having the tank deck available as a hospital, we actually put them in our own bunks."[13]

In August 1944, *LST 48* went on to participate in the invasion of southern France.

"In Normandy, the beaches have a very slight slope so when an LST went on the beach they stayed for six hours and waited for the tide to come in enough and float them off. In southern France, there is no beach so actually you ran up on what they'd call a beach and have to keep your engines running in order to hold your position there. So you can unload rather rapidly. Which we did. As we left, one of our sister ships (*LST 282*) that took our place got hit with a radio controlled bomb. It wiped her out. We figured we were just ten minutes short of being there. So that made us a pretty lucky ship."[14]

Ed and *LST 48* also participated in the Okinawa invasion (May and June 1945) and the occupation of Japan.

Minnie Stefano's future father-in-law told her that Dravo was hiring. "And I thought, well, I'll go down and see if I can get a job there. I said, What are they hiring for? And he said, 'welders.' I said, I don't know anything about welding. He said, 'But they have a school there. They'll send you over to South Side where they teach you how to weld.'

"That's what I did."[15]

Minnie's twin sister, Nellie, also worked at Dravo as a welder. Minnie recalls:

"We would sit on the Boulevard and get a ride to our job. We were in that period of our lives that our parents didn't have cars. So someone that would be working down there, one of the men would say, well I'm going past so and so, Ohio River Boulevard. Well, could we hitch a ride with you? And then that's what we did.

After work, we would stop at this one place. It was called Mancini's Café. And we'd have something to eat and we'd sing and get up and dance. Then we'd go home. Go get some sleep and then we'd go right back again.

My (future) father-in-law used to say, 'I can't believe you girls are making more money than us guys.' He was working harder because he was working on the railroad and that was hard."[16]

Minnie lived on the North Side. One day her neighbors, the Landrys, were having a party and Minnie was invited. She went and met Jim Landry. Jim went into the service and they started writing each other. The next year, in August 1943, while Jim was home on leave from the Navy, they got married. Jim was then shipped out and Minnie didn't see him for 31 months. She didn't go back to work at Dravo after she was married.

When asked if she liked welding, Minnie responded:

"Yes. It was interesting. I didn't regret one bit of it. It was an interesting area of our lives because we had to try to do what we could to help the boys in the service. You can't get more patriotic than that."[17]

Minnie worked the same shift as Ann Grindel. They became good friends. Minnie says, "I think it's just wonderful that you can have friends like that and stay friends over the years. She's really about the only one I know that we stayed friends with that long."[18]

* * * * *

Of the first 60 LSTs that Dravo was to build, five were built at its Wilmington, Delaware shipyard. In order to construct *LSTs 6, 10, 16, 21,* and *25*, the original barge-building berths and launching ways had to be reinforced and enlarged to support these larger, heavier ships. Dravo, Wilmington primarily constructed Destroyer Escorts and Landing Ships, Medium.[19]

Cliff Kincaid was a helmsman on *LST 25* and was at the invasion of Normandy on June 6, 1944. He carried coded messages from ship to ship in a small boat from the LST. About a 100 yards from the

Normandy shore, the small boat hit a mine and was blown out of the water. Cliff and the other sailors in the boat were unharmed and were able to swim to the shore of Juno Beach. "Thank God it was June 6th and not January 6th when we took our unscheduled swim."[20]

After Normandy, Cliff was sent home on leave and then went to the South Pacific. *LST 25* had a fire aboard its ship while in the South Pacific. "I guess I should thank God I'm still alive."[21]

On July 21, 1944, near Winchester, England, Lt. Dorothy Beaver, a nurse in the 30th Field Hospital, married Dr. David Pecora. Two days later, Dorothy and the 30th Field Hospital, now assigned to General Patton's Third Army, were carried by an LST to Omaha Beach. Dorothy explains, "We cared for the severely injured immediately off the front line. We lived in tents and moved as the army moved and needed us."[22]

One of the saddest memories she has of caring for the troops was "a beautiful young officer who lost both arms and legs. His spirit was so great. He kept saying - 'I am going home to my wife and two little daughters.'"[23]

The 30th Field Hospital also worked in two concentration camps. One was a woman's camp at Penig, Germany and the other was a men's camp at Ebensee, Austria. Dorothy recounts, "I had no knowledge of concentration camps. When I walked into their living conditions, I was shocked." In recent years, Dorothy has "had the honor of meeting survivors from both camps."[24]

Dorothy attended the dedication of Dravo Plaza and Points of Remembrance in Wilmington, Delaware on June 6, 1999. The Points of Remembrance are a symbolic representation of the ships that were built at Dravo, Wilmington.

Chapter Three

Large Slow Targets

Kathryn Venhoff contracted polio when she was 17 months old. It left her left leg 4 ½ inches shorter than her right. In 1926, Kathryn married Howard Wise. Her father wouldn't give Kathryn permission to marry Howard because Howard was not a Catholic, but when Kathryn turned 21, she told her father he may as well give her permission because she was going to marry Howard anyway.

Kathryn was 37 years old when she started working at the Jeffersonville Boat & Machine Co. (Jeffboat) in Jeffersonville, Indiana. Kathryn's daughter, Juanita explains:

"My father, Howard Wise, was 42 years old and decided to join the U.S. Army. He received a second lieutenant commission in the (Army) Postal Service and was immediately shipped out to the CBI (China Burma India) theater. He didn't return for two years.

No checks arrived for my mother from the government so she was forced to look for work. With no training, she was having a hard time finding employment. Some kind soul finally gave her a very good recommendation and she found a job at Jeffboat as a painter's helper. They were making LSTs and her job was prep work for the painters.

My mother eventually became the first woman painter at Jeffboat and yes, she found a lot of discrimination on the way.

She painted masts in the freezing cold, all the higher parts of the ships. She was cleared by the Navy to paint radar installations which at that time were a high security area no one knew about. They worked seven days a week sometimes. On weekends, I would stay with my grandmother."[1]

Kathryn and Juanita lived in the West End of Louisville. Kathryn car pooled to Jeffersonville with several people.

"When my mother found her job, she went to the Sisters of Loretto who had a grade and high school in our part of town. She begged them to keep me every day after school. I arrived at six in the morning and left around six at night. Thank God for those Sisters. I had been in public school because my father was not a Catholic. I entered Loretto in the fourth grade and it certainly changed my life."[2]

Kathryn joined the CIO Maritime union and was elected Secretary-Treasurer of the local union. Juanita will tell you that Kathryn "had some rather terrible experiences in this capacity. The union had several factions involved; the Communists, a criminal element, thug types. All from out of town. All vying for power and trying to access membership funds.

They once threatened to throw her out of a building window if she didn't sign checks for them. I was with her on one of these occasions. A thug named Johnson brandished a gun in a room full of union representatives. I remember she pushed me behind a chair. She went to the FBI finally but they weren't much help."[3]

Kathryn was chosen to christen *LST 867*, which she did on December 1, 1944. Her daughter, Juanita, didn't go to the christening because the Sisters wouldn't let her out of school. However, Juanita and both her parents went to the commissioning. The Wise family gave the crew a brindle Boston Bulldog which became the ship's mascot. *LST 867* performed occupation duty in the Pacific.

LST 867 Commissioning, December 18, 1944. Courtesy of: Juanita Wise Santos.

LST 867 Commissioning. Howard Wise, Kathryn Wise, Juanita Wise, Mrs. V. Lopresti, Ens. V. Lopresti. Courtesy of: Juanita Wise Santos

In 1995, Kathryn donated her coveralls and identification badge to the Smithsonian's National Museum of American History for their Women War Workers exhibit.[4]

* * * * *

The shipyard in Jeffersonville opened in 1939 as the Howard Shipyards. It is located along the Ohio River across the river from Louisville, Kentucky. The shipyard constructed 123 LSTs including *LST 507* which was sunk by a German E-boat torpedo during Exercise Tiger.

On the southern coast of England, south of Dartmouth, is a beach at Slapton Sands which has some similarities to Utah Beach. The Allies needed a place to practice for the invasion of Normandy and selected Slapton Sands. On November 4, 1943, people living in an area of approximately 30,000 acres surrounding Slapton Sands were

Jeffboat, 1944. Courtesy of: Howard Steamboat Museum, LST Collection.

ordered to evacuate. This evacuation order was allowed under the 1939 Defense Regulation and Compensation Act.[5]

Exercise Tiger was one of the training exercises for the landings on Utah Beach. The first wave of landings occurred on April 27, 1944. After the initial landings, a follow-up convoy was to land on the beach the following morning. This convoy consisted of *LSTs 58* (built at Dravo, Neville Island), *289* (built at Ambridge), *496, 499,* and *531* (built at Evansville), *511* and *515* (built at Seneca), and *507* (built at Jeffersonville). *LST 515* was at the head of the convoy and *LST 507* was the last in line.

The convoy was to be protected by the British destroyer, the HMS *Scimitar*, and a British corvette, the HMS *Azalea*.

Earlier in the evening of April 27th, the *Scimitar* was accidently rammed by a Landing Craft, Infantry (LCI) which caused a hole in the side of the destroyer. When the *Scimitar* went back to Plymouth to refuel, the ship's Captain was ordered to stay in port and have the damage repaired. Because the Captain assumed the higher authorities knew about the damaged destroyer and he was ordered to stay in port, the Captain never reported that the *Scimitar* was not going back out to help protect the LST convoy.[6]

This left only the *Azalea,* with a speed of 16 knots, to protect the convoy. *Azalea* was positioned ahead of *LST 515*. Unfortunately, due to a typographical error in orders, the LSTs were not on the correct radio frequency to communicate with the *Azalea.*[7] This meant that the Commander of the LST convoy could not talk to the Captain of the *Azalea*. The LSTs could only communicate among themselves.

Around 7:30 PM, a British staff officer was reading the signal log and realized something was missing. He called the Captain of the *Scimitar*. It took several hours to locate the Captain.[8]

Around 10:00 PM that evening, nine German E-boats or "Schnellbottes," as the Germans called them, left Cherbourg, France and started across the English channel. The E-boats had a top speed of 40 knots and a range of 700 miles.[9]

About 1:30 AM on April 28th, the Plymouth command realized that the *Scimitar* wasn't protecting the convoy and there were reports of three groups of E-boats out there. The HMS *Saladin* was ordered to join up with the LST convoy as quickly as possible. The *Saladin* was 30 miles away from the convoy and it would take at least an hour and a half to get there.[10]

About the same time the Plymouth command realized that the *Scimitar* wasn't out with the convoy, the E-boats found their first target, *LST 507*. A torpedo hit *LST 507* and it eventually sank. Two torpedoes hit *LST 531* and it sank within six minutes. A fourth torpedo hit *LST 289*, but with the help of five of its LCVPs (Landing Craft, Vehicle, Personnel) and later a French tug, it made it back to Dartmouth.[11]

Adelbert Sickley was aboard *LST 507* and recalls:

"I was a member of the Foxy 29 Medical Group. The Foxy 29 was a combat medical group and there were about 40 of us aboard the *507*. We were being transported on the *507* to land on Normandy. That was our purpose. We were to land and take in casualties. We had 40 corpsmen and two doctors that were members of the combat medical group aboard *LST 507*.

What do I remember about that night? It's pretty hard to forget it.

I remember about 1:30 *(AM)* we were called to General Quarters. I didn't really have a battle station. What I did do aboard the ship when we were going across the Atlantic, we filled magazines with ammunition. That's about the only thing I would have been doing as far as

LST 289 damage from torpedo. Courtesy of: Russ Padden.

the *507* was concerned because I didn't belong to the actual ship's company.

When General Alarm was called, I got out of bed at 1:30 and I went up toward the top deck. Before I got there, we got hit by the torpedo. I was about halfway up the ladder. The concussion of the blast threw me practically off the ladder and I was just able to barely catch myself on the railing and get my balance back on the ladder.

By the time I got out of the hatch to the main deck, there were people coming around dogging down the hatches, trying to seal off the compartments of the LST. The explosion knocked everything out. The electricity, water, everything. I saw one of the sailors holding a fire hose, the water was just barely trickling out of it because everything was shut off.

We had a lot of gasoline and ammunition aboard. We had army trucks and DUKWs and tanks. We had other amphibious craft aboard. And all of this gasoline started exploding. And pretty soon we got oil leaks from the oil that was stored for the operation of the motors of the LST. It was just like a chain reaction. The more gasoline caught fire, the more explosions, the more oil leaks, the ammunitions started exploding. People were getting hit by the ammunition or getting thrown by the explosion into the fire, catching fire.

We were ordered by this time to get down on the decks because of the danger of the flying ammunition and explosion. And stay on the deck. We did this for possibly a half hour. It was so hot, you couldn't stay on the deck anymore. But it did give me an opportunity to crawl over to the rail of the ship, to the port side of the ship. It did give me an opportunity to assess the situation and sort of make some plan as to what I was going to do because I had a pretty good feeling that we weren't going to be on that ship too long. That we were going to have to abandon ship.

I was able to spend that time assessing the situation at the same time I was watching a crew trying to get a small boat off the davit it was stored on. I saw that they were having trouble. Everything had to be done by hand. They had no electrical equipment working at all. They were trying to get this loose. They were having trouble with it. And I saw the oil surrounding the ship and the fire. The oil was on fire.

I thought my only chance was to jump down in that water when the order was given to abandon ship and get over to that small boat. It was called an LCVP, Landing Craft, Vehicle, Personnel.

A lot of those were destroyed or caught on fire. So they only had about two of them that they could get off of the ship. And the two of them would accommodate maybe 90 personnel. There were about 500 personnel or more aboard the ship. Those that didn't get killed, or didn't get burnt up or didn't drown in the bottom of the ship, all would be trying to get to those LCVPs.

We threw over everything that we could, that we thought would float. When the order was given to abandon ship, I jumped off the port side into the water. I remembered my training in boot camp. When you jump into burning oil on the surface of the water, you come back up and you splash and you splash and you go back down and you swim under water as far as you can until you have to go back up for a breath again. But when you come up, you splash with your hands to try to keep the flames away from you.

By this time I got to the small boat. I was able to pull myself up from a hanging cable into the boat. At the same time, guys that were in the boat were trying to get the thing loose yet. And they finally did get it loose. By this time, I was helping others get into the boat until we were completely filled to our maximum. That's how I got away.

But a lot of them, sailors were struggling and shouting and hollering for help. We just couldn't take any more along.

We were out in the water for about four, four and a half hours on this small boat until we were finally picked up by a British destroyer called the *Saladin*. Then we were taken back to Portland (England).

In the meantime you could see bodies floating in the water. It was just like hundreds of bodies out there in the water floating. When we were sent back to Portland, a couple of the ships had already picked up some of these bodies. And they were unloading them on the dock. When we were taken there. A lot of our friends, buddies — bodies— burnt, shot up."[12]

When asked how many of the Foxy 49 survived, Adelbert replied:

"I would say about half of them. I'd say out of our ship, about half of them were lost. Out of the *LST 531* that was sunk, only about 40 were saved. I'd say about 450 personnel all together. The one that was hit, the *289*, but not sunk, they lost about 12.

The *LST 507* was hit by one torpedo. The *531* was hit by two of them. That's why it sunk so rapidly. Within minutes it was down, six minutes, I think. The *289* was hit by one torpedo on the bow of the ship but it wasn't sunk."[13]

The LST's shallow draft made it difficult for a torpedo to hit it. Unless the torpedo is set at the surface of the water, it will not hit an LST but go under it. Adelbert explains why the German torpedoes hit the LSTs that morning. "The German E-boats that were firing that night, there were nine of them. They were firing their torpedoes at us but had them set to go under the surface of the water. Some of them missed us. I would say they spent all of their torpedoes and I think there must have been about 39 torpedoes out of the nine boats that were out there. Only about four of them hit the mark.

The German commanders finally realized that their torpedoes were missing, going under them so they did get some of them to go at surface level. But it was a little too late. They used up all their torpedoes before they got the rest of the ships.

Had they sunk all eight LSTs that were out there, there wouldn't have been a Normandy invasion on June 6th. If there would have been one at all, it would have been delayed for quite awhile. We just didn't have that many LSTs to spare."[14]

Earl Minard was an Electrician Maintenance, 2nd class on *LST 511*. He recalls:

I don't remember too much. I was just a kid. I shouldn't say I was a kid, 19, 20 years old. I know it happened April 28, 1944 at about one o'clock in the morning. I think there were eight of our ships. They're all the same, all the LSTs loaded down with army personnel and equipment.

They sounded GQ about that time. Everybody went to their stations and it wasn't long that three ships behind us, our stern, the *507* and the *531*, two of them sunk and one was hit in the rare end, it was paralyzed. It couldn't move.

It was scary ... for a young kid, you know.

The next morning, you could see on the part of England where they had several army ambulances lined for the ones who were injured, for the ones who were taken out of the water, and that kind of stuff.

We had a little problem on our ship. We had to get the soldiers to help man some of our guns in the bow because some of our gunners up there got hit. None were killed but they were injured. And it was just kind of a scary deal. Everything happened. Everybody is trying to get around. And the soldiers didn't know what to do.

The gunners on the stern of *496* opened fire. They claimed they saw one of the E-boats go between our bow and their stern. That's what we're always told. They opened fire. They hit our gunners in the bow of our ship. The gunners up there were running 40 mm guns. And they were hit.

There was only one time I was topside and I went around to the stern. I'd seen no fires. I'd seen two places where there was heavy smoke, the two ships that were sunk. You could see the smoke on the horizon. I didn't see any fire."[15]

LST 511 went on and participated in the Normandy invasion. When asked what he remembered about the Normandy invasion, Earl replied:

"There were so many ships and so much excitement. And planes and everything else. But yet, between the two of them, as I remember, what scared me worse was Exercise Tiger. I could say that about the night of that surprise attack upon us. And Normandy beach. It was so, so terrible. I was told once 5,000 ships. But I don't know if there were that many. All different kinds of ships. Exercise Tiger scared me more.

I can't even remember where I was that night. Like I said, it happened about one o'clock in the morning. I don't know if I was on watch, down in the engine room, if I was sleeping. I know we couldn't, the Navy couldn't sleep in their bunks. We got orders to stay out of our bunks and the soldiers got orders to sleep in our bunks, where they could rest. The soldiers had to have rest. They couldn't be sitting in a seat or sitting down against a wall someplace or a bulkhead somewhere. They at least had to get some rest, if they could."[16]

The typical water temperature in Lyme Bay between March and April is 8 to 11 degrees Centrigrade[17] or 46 to 52 degrees Fahrenheit. At 3:15 AM, the HMS *Saladin* rescued about 50 men clinging to the bow of one of the sunken LSTs.[18]

Meanwhile, the Skipper of *LST 515*, Lt. John Doyle, was arguing with the convoy commander about turning back to try and pick up survivors. The convoy commander was concerned that the E-boats were still out there. Finally, Doyle prevailed and at 4:15 AM, *LST 515* turned around.[19] It rescued 132 men and picked up 45 dead.[20]

The HMS *Onslow* showed up around 5 AM and also picked up survivors.[21]

The U.S. Army estimates that 749 men died in the early morning hours of April 28th. Many died of hypothermia and exhaustion. Many drowned and one cause is attributed to the incorrect wearing of the new carbon dioxide inflated single life belts. The men had not been properly instructed in the care and use of them. They were to be worn under the armpits but many of the soldiers wore them around the waist. This caused the individual to flip face first in the water and with the weight of the equipment the soldier was carrying on his back, he could not turn over.[22]

The *LST 515* returned to the Portland Harbor. In the harbor there were many LSTs flying their flags at half-mast. But it was not for the men who died that morning. Secretary of the Navy, William Franklin Knox, had also died that day at the age of 70.[23]

The dead were quickly buried in a mass grave and the survivors were told not to talk about what happened. The concern was that if the news got out, the Germans would know where the ships and troops were practicing for the Normandy Invasion. After the war, the mass grave was opened and the bodies were either moved to a new U.S. military cemetery at Cambridge, England or shipped to the United States if the next of kin requested it.[24]

But it wasn't entirely secret. Dr. David Pecora, serving in the U.S. Army Medical Corps in the U.K., wrote in his book, *Between the Raindrops*:

"The Germans announced that they had sunk two Landing Ship Tanks engaged in training on the English coast ... Late in April, our CO notified me that I would be sent on detached service with another officer and two enlisted men to accompany invasion troops on an LST and return with the wounded. He told me that I might get killed and almost apologetically explained the reason I had been chosen was that I had no dependents and I was the least well trained and therefore, the most expendable man on the surgical team.

Early in May, NIBS (Northern Ireland Base Section) canceled my orders and substituted another assignment. Apparently, my experience was not considered extensive enough for the original job. Instead I was to head another team consisting of an additional officer and ten men to set up a dispensary in the invasion area."[25]

Later, Dr. Pecora learned that the team that had taken his place on the LST on D-day had all returned safely.

When asked why Exercise Tiger was kept secret, Adelbert Sickley will tell you:

"There was a definite reason for it. For one thing, it would be an embarrassment to any high command that was in charge of the exercise. The main reason they kept it secret was the proximity of the date of April 28, 1944 to D-day which is less than six weeks. It was kept secret more or less not to provoke the enemy to discover any type of exercise that was going on. They didn't want to tip the date of the actual invasion. They didn't want to reveal it to the enemy.

In July or August, the news came out. There was a little article in the Stars and Stripes. I'm sure that General Eisenhower announced it at the time. D-day had already taken place. You know, news media follow breaking news. Once the luster of a news item wears off due to time, then the media follows the breaking news. They don't follow anything that happened six weeks ago. With D-day and our forces trying to invade Europe or trying to gain land in Europe, the media kept following that. The progress of the armed forces after D-day. That was, I think one of the factors. And then it was an embarrassment to the British and American command. They probably didn't want to be associated too much with it."[26]

Of the 251 men of the 3206th Quartermaster Service Company, 195 were killed and nine were wounded in Exercise Tiger. They were aboard *LST 531*. There is a memorial to the 3206th in the courthouse square of Mexico, Missouri. Many of the 3206th were from Audrain County, Missouri. Highway 54 leading to Mexico, Missouri is named the Exercise Tiger Expressway.

A granite memorial stands on the beach of Slapton Sands to honor the men who died in Exercise Tiger. The second paragraph of the inscription reads:

"May these men rest in the knowledge that the lessons of this tragedy added significantly to the ability of the Allies to carry out the successful invasion of Normandy on June 6, 1944. May these soldiers and sailors be remembered for their supreme sacrifice for the Allied cause in World War II."

Chapter Four

The Navy Yards

Five Navy Yards (Boston; New York; Norfolk, Virginia; Philadelphia; and Charleston, South Carolina) built 94 LSTs. Of these five yards, only the Boston Navy Yard laid keels for LSTs after 1942. The Boston yard built 44 LSTs.

Shipyard welders were under the Naval Administration's Labor Group IV(b). In March 1943, only 5.5 percent of the entire Labor Group IV(b) of these five shipyards were women.[1] Given these statistics, it is not surprising that the author was unable to locate women who were welders on the Navy Yard built LSTs.

But she did receive letters from men who sailed on Navy Yard built LSTs.

Art Hamilton served on *LST 980*, built at the Boston Navy Yard, from 1944 to 1946. *LST 980* sailed to England in April 1944. While it was docked in London, waiting for the Normandy invasion, it survived some of the heaviest "Buzz Bomb" attacks.[2]

LST 980 participated in the Normandy invasion and was hit by a 125 pound dud bomb which penetrated its hull and two bulkheads, injuring a man. She shuttled between England and France, carrying troops and equipment to France and returning with prisoners of war. She returned to the U.S. on February 15, 1945 and was assigned to training activities along the east coast.[3]

Landing Ships on one of the invasion beaches during the first days of Operation Overload, June 1944. LST 310 was built at the Boston Navy Yard. Collection of the Evansville Museum of Arts, History, and Science.

The Boston Navy Yard was established in 1800 and closed in 1974. Today, thirty acres of it is part of the Boston National Historical Park.

Adrian Albrecht was an Engineering Yeoman on *LST 982*. "I watched them build *LST 982* in the Boston shipyards in 1944, thinking the war would be over by the time they completed our ship. But lo and behold, in about four weeks we were ready to go to sea.

We were sent to Swansea, Wales and prepared for the invasion of France. We made 24 trips carrying soldiers and supplies to France from England and hauling prisoners back to England."[4]

LST 982 returned to Norfolk, Virginia in January 1945 and the ship was painted in camouflage colors. Unlike its sister ship, *LST 980*, it did not stay in the U.S. for the rest of the war. It sailed for the Pacific and participated in the Okinawa invasion. *LST 982* also performed occupation duty.

* * * * *

Of the eight LSTs built at the New York Navy Yard, which was located in Brooklyn, three did not survive. Peter Maurin was on one of them, *LST 313*. His ship was hit by a bomb at Gela, Sicily. Peter recalls:

"We sailed from New York on April 28, 1943 with the tank deck loaded with tank destroyers and *LCT 444* on top deck. It was a rough journey across the North Atlantic in the winter time. The ocean was very rough. When we were in the bottom of a wave, all that we could see was water, water, water. Many sailors were sea sick the whole trip. We arrived in time to do more preparations and beaching exercises for our trip to Sicily.

I was given the job of being the Pointer, firing a 20 mm anti-aircraft gun on the port side amidships. An ME (Messerschmidt) came out of the sun but I could not see it until it dropped the bomb. I fired a burst, but did not fire any more for fear of injuring the soldiers on the beach. The bomb hit amidships with soldiers in their vehicles ready to embark as soon as we hit the beach.

We were ordered to abandon ship. I had to get to the starboard side to where the cargo net was hanging and crawl down into the water. Then I was rescued by Phillip Reymous who manned the boat hook and pulled me and other shipmates aboard to safety. Our LCVP picked us up after awhile in the water and took us to a ship for shipment to North Africa."[5]

LST 313 on fire after being hit by a bomb from a Messerschmidt near Geta, Sicily on July 10, 1943. Source: HyperWar: U.S. Navy in WWII.

Afterwards, the crew of the *LST 313* was sent back to the U.S. Most of its crew, including its Executive Officer, was assigned to *LST 286*, built in Pittsburgh by American Bridge Company.

Roger Noreen was assigned to *LST 312* when it was commissioned in Brooklyn. It was involved in both the invasion of Africa and the invasion of Italy. Returning to England in the winter of 1943, it was in the first wave to hit Normandy and took the British into Omaha Beach. After making several trips across the Channel, it went back to London and moored next to *LST 384* at the Naval Amphibious Base. Roger recalls:

"We went up the Thames to London to have our engines worked on. While there, the *312* and *384* were moored side by side. We got hit right between us with a Buzz bomb, which did a great deal of damage to both vessels, with a loss of eight of our fellow shipmates. We were made seaworthy and went to Birmingham, England to be repaired."[6]

Roger went back to the U.S. and was assigned to *LST 1108*, built at Evansville, Indiana. "We were in the Philippines when they dropped the Bomb on Japan. We were ready for the invasion of Japan. Thank the Lord they dropped the bomb."[7]

It was an LST similar to Roger's that war correspondent Ernie Pyle rode on to Anzio. Although Pyle never identified the ship number, the LST he rode on to Anzio had been the one he had been on in Bizerte, Tunisia. Pyle wrote about his LST cruise and it is included in his book, *Brave Men.* In this chapter he wrote:

"The LST isn't such a glorious ship to look at. It is neither sleek nor fast nor impressively big - no bigger than an ocean freighter - and yet it is a good ship and the crews aboard LSTs are proud of them."[8]

Later in the chapter he describes the commander of the ship, Lt. Kahrs, maneuvering into the Anzio harbor.

"There he stood, far from home, worming his ship into a half-wrecked harbor with shells passing a few feet over his head. And he did it with complete absorption and confidence. Men can do strange and great things when they have to do them."[9]

Ernie Pyle survived the war in Europe. Unfortunately, he was killed by a Japanese sniper's machine gun bullet on April 18, 1945. It was two days after the Marines landed on Ie Shima, a small island west of Okinawa. When the men and women who were fighting in World War II heard the news, they silently cried. They had lost one of their best friends.

* * * * *

The Norfolk Navy Yard is the Navy's oldest shipyard. It's original name was the Gosport Shipyard. It was renamed in 1862 after the largest city in the area, Norfolk. However, it is located in Portsmouth, Virginia. Out of the twenty LSTs that were built there, three did not survive the war.

Bill Johnson started out on *LST 208*, built in Seneca, Illinois. He will tell you that they were proud of their ship and kept it clean. But a few days after *LST 208* arrived at Bizerte, Tunisia they directed *LST 208* to pull along side *LST 349*, built at Norfolk, and the crews were to exchange ships. Bill explains:

"The *349* had been there since March and was a rusty bucket. The crew's quarters were filthy. We didn't sleep in the crews quarters until we had taken all the canvas off the bunks and scrubbed them. Painted the quarters after scrubbing them. We slept in the side compartments during that time.

They had a monkey. There was monkey doo doo on top of all the port battle plates in the wheelhouse. Trails up the stanchions from him. What a mess to clean.

Before we left the U.S., we had supplied the ship with plenty of paint and repair parts. The men put much of this into sea bags and took it over the sides into the *349*! So we had paint and parts to repair what needed to be. We were just to take our personal things. But, who

LST 349 aground off Isla de Ponza, Italy. Source: LST Home Port website.

An Army Piper Cub observation plane takes off from an LST. Source: U.S. Naval Historical Center.

knows what is in sea bags and who is counting how many times you cross the deck."[10]

LST 349 participated in the Salerno invasion and the Anzio invasion. On February 26, 1944, after 13 trips to Anzio, it was sunk in a storm.

At the Sicily and Anzio landings, on some of the LSTs, "they built a wooden launch deck on the front area and would launch Piper Cubs from them for reconnaissance work. They couldn't land on the deck, so they were then abandoned and let crash. The pilot would be picked up."[11]

Bill has served on Attack Transports, the USS *Wisconsin*, and a destroyer. He will tell you, "The LST is in my blood. They were great to serve on. We had a great Skipper. Mostly good officers. None of the bridge crew smoked. Unusual. But were they ever rough riding in a storm. The Med is very choppy in storms. There were times we had to tie ourselves in our bunks to keep from bouncing out!"[12]

It was probably *LST 340* that Don Cubley was on once, off of Tinian Island. *LST 340* was grounded on July 29, 1944. Don explains:

"We had invaded Saipan, first of all, then waited to see if we, 2nd Marine Division, would be needed in the capture of Guam. We weren't, so proceeded to Tinian ... Saipan had six varieties of malaria. Evidently, I got something and by the time we had captured half of the island (Tinian), I became very weak.

We had come to these islands at sugar cane harvest. Most all of the leaves had been burned and were slippery. I had difficulty getting back on my feet after falling so I was eventually sent from the battle.

As I travelled toward the north end of the island, a typhoon began to blow from that direction. The doors were open and the ramp down and I managed to get aboard while the LST bucked against the huge waves. The floor inside was well covered with wounded Marines on stretchers. The waves put the LST upon the reef and it rocked to and fro all night. It was perched to stay.

The following morning, I abandoned the LST. A line was stretched from the LST to a tug boat which kept a tight line. An LCVP came along side to take on riders. The waves were raising high the LCVP and dropping it low. I would try to jump into it as it came up. I jumped, it dropped below and came up to meet me while I was still in the air. I hit the plywood floor hard but didn't make a hole. I made it back to Saipan safely."[13]

LST 340 was refloated on August 13, 1944 and towed to Saipan. On October 20, 1944, it was reclassified as IX-196 and named *Spark*. Four days later it was decommissioned.[14]

* * * * *

Fourteen LSTs were constructed at the Philadelphia Navy Yard. The Navy Yard operated from 1801 until late 1996. It is the birthplace of today's most famous LST - *LST 325*.

LST 325 was transferred to Greece and served in the Greek Navy until December 1999. In 2000, she was acquired by USS Ship Memorial, Inc. It took about three and a half months and over 50 people to get her ready to sail across the Atlantic. On November 14, 2000, *LST 325* left Crete. Twenty-eight crew members who were either veterans of World War II or the Korean War and one photographer made the entire voyage from Crete to Mobile, Alabama. They arrived in Mobile on January 10, 2001.[15]

In September 1945, Captain Fred M. Earle wrote an article entitled "*Employment of Women in the Navy Yards*." He ended the article with the following:

"Women in shipyards have been invaluable. We could not have got along without them. Their contribution will be long remembered by a grateful nation."[16]

Chapter Five

Bring It Back

When John Massey and the other crew members arrived to pick up *LST 830* in Ambridge, Pennsylvania in the Fall of 1944, they were greeted by the all women crew who built it. The women gave John and his crew members a small bag with items such as a razor, blades, toothbrush, etc. The head woman made a brief speech and said "We built it. Take it over and bring it back." The LST crew did just that.[1]

Virginia Cogley was building walkie talkies in 1943 when she heard about the shipyard. "They paid more money at the time. A couple of us went together to go down there and get a job."[2]

Virginia was living in Pittsburgh and took a bus to the shipyard. Later, she would get a ride. Virginia was sent to Ambridge High School to learn how to weld.

Virginia recalls, " They never let the women work on the outside hull. We worked on the floors on the inside of the ship. We worked on the gun turrets. The galvanized metal in the kitchen we worked with was pretty rough work. If you got any hot rods, it would go straight through."[3]

Virginia was on one of the ships that they launched. "So many times if you were handy when they had a ship, the welders who would be in that section of the shipyard, would get to be on it."[4]

One day Virginia was asked to go to the American Bridge Company's office. "There was a man by the name of Mr. Benson. He was an artist and he picked me out of a bunch of women going to work one day. I had to pose for him and he did a picture of me with charcoal pencil. It was all black and white and I had an 8 by 10 of it."[5]

When Virginia was 15, she met 16 year old Louis Wittman at a roller rink. During the war, Louis was in the Air Force. After the war, Virginia and Louis married.

Virginia worked at the shipyard until she was laid off in 1945. Then she and other coworkers went to work for Jones and Laughlin Steel Corporation for several months.

* * * * *

American Bridge Company, a subsidiary of U.S. Steel, built and operated the Ambridge shipyard. The first LST keel was laid in September 1942, only four and one half months after American Bridge received its letter of authorization from the Navy.

To expedite construction of the yard, the company purchased and utilized used materials and machinery. This included the use of steel from a structure dismantled at the Tubular Alloy Steel Corporation Plant in Gary, Indiana, to construct the east aisle of the three-aisled plate shop. The east aisle was equipped with four overhead electric traveling cranes from the same source. A warehouse was constructed from steel obtained from two buildings of the Gary, Indiana Ordinance Plant and steel which formerly housed the forge shop of American Bridge's Gary Plant was used to build a sheet metal and pipe shop. Of the 9,300 tons of structural steel required for the shipyard structure, over 35% was used material.[6]

122 LSTs were built in Ambridge.

An acquaintance of Lois Leseman from the Mars, Pennsylvania area heard that American Bridge Company was hiring women welders. "We were both new brides with husbands in the service," Lois explains. "We applied for a job and were immediately hired. We went to welding school and I started to vertical weld at the plant in January 1943. One night, the foreman said to me, 'you're not going to weld tonight, you're going to school.' They sent me to class for overhead welding at the plant. They had a school right at the plant."[7]

The plant was where the precut steel plates were welded into ship sections. The welded ship sections, called sub-assemblies, were then placed on 50 ton capacity trailers and hauled to the ship assembling berths.[8]

"You were exhausted by the time you got home," explains Lois. "It was not only that you went to work and welded. You had to find your machine, have the men move it, then take all your paraphernalia up in these sections, and those sections were small in the aft end.

It was cold, right along the river. You would weld one spot and put your back up against it to keep warm. The only heat we had was a barrel that had fire in it. If they saw anybody standing around that barrel, it wouldn't take the boss long to tell you to keep moving. There was no heat in that building at all."[9]

On Navy Day, October 27, 1943, Lois was the launch sponsor of *LST 286*. She broke the bottle of champagne on the bow of the *286* as it slid into the Ohio River. Her aide was also a welder, Wanda Olbeter.

Asked how she was selected, Lois explains, "One day when I was working, the foreman came and said, 'I want you to go up to the office.' I said, 'what for.' He said, 'It's confidential.' So I went up and the big wheels told me what they wanted me to do."[10]

Lois Leseman, holding flowers, at the Christening of LST 286. On her right is her aide, Wanda Olbeter. Courtesy of: Lois Leseman.

LST 286 Launching on October 27, 1943. Courtesy of: Lois Leseman.

Lois had worked on *LST 286* and "they thought it should be someone that really contributed to the building of it."[11]

Lois was allowed to choose her aide to christen the ship. Wanda did flat welding and was not in the same section as Lois. "She was married and had a five year old daughter at that time. I stayed overnight at her house one night. She was a nice person and this is why I chose her. She was a down to earth person."[12]

After *LST 286* was launched, *LST 282* went on it's trial run. The *282* crashed landed on the Ohio River's shore below Aliquippa. Paint had dripped from a painter's brush on the fuse connection behind the switchboard and caused a fuse on the switchboard in the electrical steering control to burn out. "That's why we have test runs," commented a Navy officer. "It's a whole lot better that that fuse burned out in the Ohio - than someday when we'll be driving shoreward to establish a beachhead under enemy fire." The LST backed out of the bank and resumed her way up river.[13]

If *LST 282* had a bad day on its test run, it had a much worse day 10 months later. *LST 282* survived its participation in the invasion of Normandy. It was used as a hospital ship and shuttled soldiers and equipment to Utah Beach and casualties to Portsmouth, England. On June 8, 1944, it went to Omaha Beach and ran into one of the spikes the Germans had placed along the beach under the water. The spike put a hole in the LST and prevented the use of one of its engines. It was towed to Portsmouth and repaired in dry dock.[14]

LST 282 proceeded to the Invasion of Southern France carrying 500 Army personnel that would go onto the beaches. Throughout the day on August 15, 1944, it was anchored less than a mile off the coast of St. Raphael. At around 8:20 PM, *PC-551* flashed a visual signal, "Proceed to the Beach Immediately." "Expedite." Ten minutes later it received a red alert over the radio.[15] It was 200 feet from the beach when a German glider bomb penetrated its main deck and exploded under the main deck.[16] Lt. Gilbert, the skipper, ordered hard left rudder, which kept the exploding LST from moving in among the LSTs already lined up on the beach. *LST 282* ran aground on some rocks in front of a resort home.[17]

Lt. Ralph Adams became the Commanding Officer of *LST 286*. Lt. Adams and many of the crew of the *LST 286* had served on *LST 313* (built at New York Navy Yard) when it had been bombed and sunk by a German plane in the invasion of Sicily on July 10, 1943.

For the invasion of Normandy, like its sister ship the *LST 282, LST 286* was outfitted to receive wounded and dead soldiers. There were Army Surgeons on Board and one of the forward lockers, on the tank deck, was used for a morgue. They returned to Portland-Weymouth, England and on June 10th, 70 Allied and 10 German wounded soldiers and four soldiers who had died were unloaded. For the rest of the month of June, *LST 286* shuttled several times between Normandy and England, picking up casualties and returning with army equipment and personnel.[18]

In mid-July, *LST 286* was ordered to go to the Mediterranean. It went to Naples harbor, loaded on vehicles and personnel of the U.S. Army, Third Division, and headed out to join the convoy for the Invasion of Southern France. After proceeding out of the harbor and turning north, a PT boat passed close to its starboard side. In it was Winston Churchill with his cigar and V for Victory sign.[19]

For the initial invasion on August 15th, *LST 286* was at Cavalaire Bay. She shuttled back once to Italy and then a few times between southern France and Algiers. On one of her trips, she went to San Raphael and some of the crew went over to look at the burned out *LST 282*.[20]

On Thanksgiving Day, 1944, *LST 286* headed back to the U.S. The ship left the U.S. on March 17, 1945 for the Pacific. It performed occupation duty in the Pacific and returned to San Francisco on January 16, 1946.[21]

When Lois Leseman began working at the Ambridge shipyard, she shared a ride with the woman who had told her about the job. Unfortunately, this didn't last long.

"She left me one night to go out with someone in Ambridge. I was stranded in Ambridge. So I went to the gate and told the watchman what happened. He said, 'Just wait here. I know two men that travel to Evans City. I don't think they've gone yet.' So that's how I got home that night.

Then I rode with them until I could make other arrangements."[22]

Other arrangements was traveling two hours to work by bus from Callery, Pennsylvania to Ambridge. She worked an 8-hour shift and took another two hour bus ride to return home. "Believe me, those buses weren't what they are today. Half of the time there was no heat."[23]

She didn't want to live in Ambridge and lived with her sister-in-law's family. It was her sister-in-law that convinced Lois to quit. Mine Safety Appliance was within walking distant of her home so she

John Massey's Amphibious Patch.

worked there on an assembly line making gas masks until the war ended.[24]

On *LST 830*, John Massey was a coxswain for the LCVP (Landing Craft, Vehicle, Personnel) it carried. In the Battle of Okinawa, six of the sailors were wounded. John returned with *LST 830* to Lake Charles, Louisiana and he has never seen it since.[25]

Lois and Bob Leseman formed a metal fabrication shop, ALY Construction, on May 1, 1957. They also owned Complex Components, Inc., which built electrical panels. Lois started South Butler Construction, Inc. in 1963. Lois took over ALY in 1987 when Bob was killed in an auto accident. She managed the company until 2001.

Today, the company is known as ALY Fabrication, Inc. and is run by Lois' daughter Linda, and Linda's husband.[26]

Chapter Six

We're Saving Your Country

Mary Rossetti was at a skating rink in Revere, Massachusetts when the Japanese bombed Pearl Harbor. When she arrived home, family and friends "were gathered there deeply shocked by the unexpected news." Although only 15, she promised herself that she would either do defense work or join the Service as soon as she was old enough.[1]

Mel Smith, who later served on *LST 919*, witnessed the attack on Pearl Harbor. He was on a large hill above Pearl Harbor.

"I was just coming off shift of 12 midnight to 8:00 AM as a welder for Morrison Knudsen Construction, where we worked on a very large project, welding on underground fuel storage tanks that fuel for the Pacific fleet", he explains. "The workers knocked off work at 7:50 AM, allowing us 10 minutes to walk to the portal of the tunnel, where upon as we walked out into the road at the portal at 7:55 AM and looked down upon the harbor below us. The Jap planes were flying in at mast height of the ships, dropping their torpedoes and strafing and bombing.

We could not accept what we were witnessing. One could hear all around, maneuvers, maneuvers. There were several dozen men changing shift at that area. No one could believe the Japs were bombing the hell out of our fleet and Hickham Air Force Base, with only a fence dividing it and Pearl.

Only one Jap plane came close to where we were on the side of that large hill. We could see his face very plainly as he flew by almost at eye level and the large rising sun logo on the side of his plane. He could have gave only a burst or two with his machine guns and mowed a lot of us onlookers down, however, he did not. I reckon he was saving his ammo for strafing the military targets.

It was only a few minutes before the smoke from the burning ships and oil burning on the water was so thick, we could no longer see the ships in the harbor, only the deafening blasts when the torpedoes and bombs hit their targets."[2]

On March 11, 1942, under orders from President Franklin D. Roosevelt, General Douglas MacArthur boarded *PT 41* and left the Philippines. A few days later, the world would hear his famous words, "I shall return."[3]

Mary Rossetti didn't have to wait long to keep her promise. She was a senior in high school in January of 1943 when a notice came around in school that if anyone wanted to leave school to either go into the Service or do defense work, they would be guaranteed a diploma in June. Since she was only 16, she was too young to go into the Service. Instead, she went to welding school.[4]

For three months, Mary attended class at the New England Welding Labs in the Back Bay of Boston. In March of 1943, she graduated as a Navy Tested Welder.[5]

Welders were supposed to be 18 when they worked in the shipyard. But Mary explains,

"We were supposed to be. But that day we went to the U.S. employment office looking for a job. Nobody wanted to hire us because my girlfriend was 17 and I was 16. Well, we happened to run into a representative from Bethlehem Steel. She called the President of

Beth-Hingham Shipyard. Courtesy of: Martin Cohn, Trustee, Hingham Shipyard Historical Foundation

Bethlehem Steel. He said 'Grab them. They're graduates.' So that's how we got the job."[6]

Bethlehem Steel received a major contract to construct Destroyer Escorts. But it's shipyards were at capacity and so in February 1942, construction began on the "Beth-Hingham" shipyard. The shipyard was located on 150 acres along Hewitt's Cove and it would include a steel mill. Don Rand's Dude Ranch and Jimmy Lahood's restaurant were torn down. In the video, "*Remembering the Hingham Shipyard*", Joe Landrey recalls that they only gave Jimmy Lahood about 15 minutes notice. The dishes and the utensils were set out on the table for lunch but Jimmy was not allowed to take anything.[7]

Ninety-five LSTs would be constructed at Beth-Hingham.

"My first day there was frightening", Mary will tell you. "I worked in a Steel Mill where they assembled all the ships parts, such as the hull, decks, etc. before putting them together on the docks. This Steel Mill had to be the noisiest place in the world! Cranes were running over our heads all day, chippers were cutting out welder's errors, steel plates were clanging and banging continuously. I went home with the biggest headache!

That didn't discourage me. I was determined to do the job I promised myself I could do and I did it for 2 full years!"[8]

For two years, Mary traveled 30 miles from East Boston to the shipyard. "Transportation was low class but lots of fun. My driver bought a "32" Reo in a junkyard for $35.00. One of our male passengers bought a funeral Limo. When he drove us - we rode in class!"[9]

After a few months in the Steel Mill, Mary was transferred to work on the docks. By this time, it was winter and the temperatures occasionally went below zero degrees. She wore "heavy long underwear, flannel shirts and dungarees, two pairs of socks and steel toed safety shoes, and long suede leather gloves. Over all that we wore suede leather jackets to keep our clothing from getting burned. To cover our heads we wore a kerchief tied in a knot like a turban and a cap over that, and of course, a Welder's Helmet."[10]

"It was very, very cold where we worked. All the ships were wide open ... and the water would freeze over. There would be ice flows. There were otters out there swimming around. That's how cold it was."[11]

"We took our coffee and lunch breaks out on the docks, even in winter. We had several small stores and lunch stands where we could buy coffee, candy, and food. In the parking area, temporary stores were set up where we could buy work clothes and shoes. This was no Bonwit Tellers!"[12]

The welder's equipment was kept in a heavy steel tool box that was stored in the docks next to the ships. "Each time we were transferred to a new ship, we had to move our equipment with us. That's when some men showed no mercy. They didn't always help us carry that from one ship to another. It sure was a heavy load for a frail young kid like myself - but again I did it!"[13]

"Most of the men I worked with were gentlemen - they would help me and teach me new methods of welding."[14]

Mary worked on a "30-day Wonder." "That's what they called one of mine that I worked on. It was built in 30 days. It was one of the first LSTs. That's when we worked three weeks in a row, 10 hours a day. We worked 7 days a week."[15]

"Each ship looked beautiful when finished. Before it left for its destination, a crew of officers and sailors occupied the ships for about a week. On the day of departure we would stand on the docks to watch them leave - we were proud of our work!"[16]

One day, Mary and her friend, Elaine, went into a Boston department store wearing their welding clothes. "You know the women in there were down on us. Oh yes- Like we were trash. I said excuse me, we're saving your country, if you don't mind."[17]

At the shipyard, Mary became friends with Marion, Fran, and Bernice Fisher. After the war, the Fisher's brother, Frank, came home from the service and the sisters introduced him to Mary. Mary and Frank married in 1947. Mary will tell you "The war patterned my life."[18]

Joseph St. John joined the army in September 1939 and ended up in the Philippines in the fall of 1941. Unlike MacArthur, his squadron did not leave the Philippines in March 1942. Instead, on the day the Philippines surrendered to the Japanese, St. John and a few other soldiers boarded a sailboat, hoping to sail to Australia. They never made it. Seven days later the boat capsized and they were still off the coast of the Philippines.[19]

St. John joined an organized guerilla force, the United States Forces in the Philippines, which was mostly composed of Filipinos. St. John agreed to run a watcher station for the Navy on Leyte.[20] In his book, *Leyte Calling*, St John describes how the Japanese came looking for him, his Filipino radio operator, and three other soldiers. He describes hiding under a log for hours, not moving because the Japanese were close by, while being bitten by ants and then the leeches arrived.[21]

On October, 17, 1944, St. John saw the American minesweepers come into Leyte Gulf. A few days later, he saw another type of ship.

"The ships were out there the morning of October 20, too. But there was something different. At first I could not tell what it was; then the ships got closer, and I saw they were different from the others. They were a kind of ship I had never seen before, funny-looking ships with the cabin and superstructure all aft and nothing but a cargo deck forward of the cabin.

I had never seen anything like those ships. They looked as though any minute they would tip over backward and sink.

Later I learned they were the LST's, the ships that can carry a whole company of men and God knows how many vehicles right up to a beach and let the trucks roll off with the men in them. The Navy did not have anything like that when I left Oahu."[22]

On the day that St. John first saw an LST, General MacArthur stepped off a landing craft in knee deep water and waded to the Leyte shore. He walked across the sand to a waiting microphone. He took the headset and said "People of the Philippines, I have returned."[23]

151 LSTs arrived at Leyte Gulf. Nine of them had been built at Beth-Hingham. Because the LSTs could travel only about two hundred miles a day, those LSTs that were harbored at Hollandia on the northern coast of New Guinea would take six days to travel to Leyte. Those harbored at Finschhafen, the southeast coast of New Guinea, would take 10 days to travel to Leyte. MacArthur's return to the Philippines presented the military planners with some major logistical problems.[24]

Fran and Marion Fisher were working at the Howard and Foster shoe factory, making shoes for the Navy. Their brother-in-law, Joseph Smith, was a shipfitter at the Hingham Shipyard and told them that welders were needed at the shipyard. The Fisher sisters had a hard time getting a release from the shoe factory because it was also a defense plant. Fran was 18 and Marion was 20 when the shipyard hired them.[25]

Fran describes welding school. "That was scary because if you looked at the welder's rod and you struck an arc without your helmet on, you could get a flash. That was a very painful eye infection. I had one, and my sister had a couple."[26]

Frances Fisher Catrabone, 1941.

Fran also remembers the cold winters working there. "Through the winter months it was freezing on the boats. We had to put Kotex (sanitary pads) in our boots because our feet were so cold."[27]

"We had to wear heavy suede jackets, and when welding over your heads, sometimes the hot steel would drop inside, which we have a few scars on our chests from."[28]

* * * * *

The Battle of Leyte Gulf, which occurred between October 23rd and October 26th, 1944 has been described as "the greatest naval engagement ever fought", "the largest naval battle in history", and the "greatest sea fight". Nearly two hundred thousand men participated in the battle. Dozens of ships were sunk, and thousands of men died.[29] Many more men would have died had not the Japanese commander, Admiral Kurita, stopped his attack on October 25th, turned around, and headed away from Leyte Gulf.

Rear Admiral Sprague, commander of one of the escort carrier groups wrote in his after-action report:

"The failure of the enemy...to wipe out all vessels of this task unit can be attributed to our successful smoke-screen, our torpedo counterattack, continuous harassment of the enemy by bomb, torpedo, and strafing air attacks, timely maneuvers, and the definite partiality of Almighty God."[30]

But a new horror appeared at the Battle of Leyte Gulf that would kill many more sailors and sink many more American ships. Japan had been saved in 1274 and again in 1281 from Kublai Khan's invasion by the arrival of Pacific typhoons. Because of these events, a legend arose that the Japanese were favored by the gods and that they were protected by the "divine wind", or in Japanese, by the kamikaze.[31]

As a result of heavy losses of Japanese aircraft in the Formosa air battle and American air strikes on the Philippines before the Leyte landing that destroyed many aircraft, Japanese air strength was depleted. Vice Admiral Takijiro Onishi, commander of the Japanese First Air Fleet, made the decision to "organize suicide attack units composed of Zero fighters armed with bombs, with each plane to crash-dive into an enemy carrier."[32]

Although there had been pilots before this that made a decision to crash their plane into a ship when they realized their plane would not survive, this was the first time that suicide tactics would be "officially sanctioned by the commander of an air unit." " It was the first time that pilots would be trained, briefed, and sent into the air with the expressed expectation that they would deliberately kill themselves in the service of their country."[33]

Kenneth (Bud) York served aboard *LST 919*, which was built at Hingham. His ship was one of the "30-Day Wonders." *LST 919*

LST 919 and LST 922 at Leyte, 1944. Source: LST Home Port website.

sailed in convoy to Leyte with Army Signal Corps units aboard. Bud remembers:

"We went in there on the fourth day. They had invaded the island four days before we went there. The Japanese were just getting organized about that time. When we got into the harbor, and before we hit the beach, there were 47 Japanese airplanes in the air. I don't know how anyone could have counted them. But that was the rumor that there were 47 of them. They just flew around like a bunch of buzzards. They didn't fly in any formation like our planes did. They just flew around, it reminded you of a bunch of buzzards. That's when they really got into the kamikazes. In fact I never heard of any kamikaze pilots until that day.

They'd just pick out a ship and they would try to bomb it first. And if they couldn't hit a ship with a bomb - they were not very good at bombing, they were terrible at that - they'd say they couldn't hit a cow in the butt with their bombs - then they would just crash dive into the ship. That was pretty scary. When you see a plane crash right into a ship, you didn't know what was going on.

We shot down one airplane. At that particular time, I was not on a gun station. I was on what they called a forward collision party. Our job was to repair any damage that was done by a bomb. So the Lieutenant told me to go around and uncover the ventilators. They were just round stacks that stuck up through the main deck out of the tank deck because when they started vehicles on the tank deck it created a lot of carbon monoxide from the fumes of the exhaust. So they had to ventilate the tank deck to get some air down there, until they could open those bow doors and get the ramps down and get traffic moving in and out of the tank deck.

They had a canvas top on all these ventilators and I was supposed to go around and uncover them, take the canvas off so they could pump air down there. Of course we had troops on there, the invading troops, the Army. There was a Lieutenant that came running across what we call the quarter deck, that's one deck above the main deck, and he was yelling to the troops, the Army guys. He said "Hit the deck. Hit the deck." And he was pointing off to his left, up toward the front of the ship.

Well, I was at a vantage point to see that. I was looking right at that airplane and I could just see the fire coming out of the machine guns. He was shooting the machine guns, and he was coming right directly towards us and I thought oh my God, I have to get down off of here. I just dropped down and there was an Army jeep parked as close to that ventilator as it could get. And I got down. Of course our guns were shooting at this airplane.

This airplane is what the Japanese called a light bomber. It was called a Betty bomber. They named their bombers after women and their pursuit planes they named them after men.

I just got down underneath that jeep as close as I could. I got my head, I put it into my helmet and my face right up against the tire of that jeep. Our guns that are going off just vibrated the whole ship. They were loud. It was deafening.

When our guns stopped and I could come out from under that jeep, I looked off and I saw this airplane going by the side of us, real low. He was off on our left side, the port side. He was going from the front of the ship towards the back of the ship. One of our bow guns, 40 mm, got it. He was out of control. He was going right towards the water and he just crashed right into the water, a little ways behind our ship and to our left.

At that time we hadn't even hit the beach yet to unload. When we did get lined up on the beach, that afternoon, I don't know what time it was, it seemed pretty late in the day. Where we were beached, our position was the first ship right on the end. There was a torpedo bomber. I think they are just a one engine bomber. But they carry a torpedo on each side, on each wing. They come in from the side and they drop them. They skip across the water.

This airplane came in, we were kind of on a curve of the island. This thing just came around that corner and he dropped his torpedo. He was a little bit late in dropping it. I don't know whether he just didn't see us in time. But anyway he was a little bit late in dropping that torpedo and it landed on the other side of our ship. It hit the sand. In other words the water wasn't deep enough where he dropped it. When he dropped the torpedo it was like dropping it straight down. It went off. It blew water sky high.

There had been a ship in that vacant space where he dropped that torpedo. But the ship was gone. It had fully unloaded and backed off from the beach. But we weren't unloaded yet."[34]

On December 12th, *LST 919* departed Leyte for Mindoro, Philippines. The next day, Bud witnessed a kamikaze crashing into the light cruiser, USS *Nashville*, killing 133 men and wounding 190. The *Nashville* was just off the starboard beam, the right side of *LST 919*, about midship. Arriving at Mindoro on December 15th, Bud witnessed the crash diving of kamikazes into *LSTs 472* (built at Kaiser, Vancouver) and *738* (built at Dravo, Neville Island).

"When we were loading to go to Mindoro," Bud explains. "They were loading all that aviation gasoline on our main deck. I can't recall how many 55 gallon drums of aviation gasoline we had. They just loaded them on the main deck. Our tank deck was full of them too. One of the officers, I just learned this two or three years ago at one of our reunions, told us that the Commander of our Flotilla told the officers that our chances of returning from that invasion was one in three. And I said, I'm damn glad you didn't share that information with us enlisted men because I was scared as it was.

But you see all that gasoline loading all around you and you think, oh my God, one piece of hot metal, one piece of shrapnel and you're in

LST 738 after kamikaze attack. Collection of Admiral Thomas C. Kinvaid, USN. Source: U.S.Naval Historical Center.

LST 472 after kamikaze attack. Source: HyperWar: U.S. Navy in World War II.

the middle of an inferno. And that's what happened to the *472*."[35]

LST 472 and *738* did make it into the harbor. "They were still burning that night when we left. God, it was an awful fire."[36]

On January 3rd, *LST 919* sailed in convoy towards Lingayen Gulf, Philippines. It carried members of General MacArthur's staff and their equipment. En route, on January 7th, kamikazes crashed into the Attack Transport *Callaway* and *LST 912* (built at Hingham). Bud recalls:

"Oh yes. That was one night. I remember that attack transport getting hit. I can't remember how many men were on there but there were a lot of fatalities from that one. I think that convoy was about 35 miles ahead of us.

This definitely happened at night. We saw the explosions from it. It lit the sky up. But at that time, we didn't know what was going on. The next morning ... now we always had to stand general quarters every morning at sunrise and every night at sunset. And the reason for that was because the Japanese favorite trick was to come out of the sun. You had to look into the sun and you couldn't see them coming.

So every night at sunset and every morning at sunrise we had to be at general quarters. This time, though, they had transferred me off the forward collision party to a gun position. And I was a pointer on what they called a 20 mm. That's one where you're strapped into your gun. You're the trigger man on that.

A lot of those guys were blown overboard. And they were still in the water. They'd been in the water all night long. When we came along, we were standing watch at general quarters and these guys, they would be in their life jackets out there in the water. And they were yelling. You could hear them screaming at us. Of course, they were wanting us to pick them up. None of the convoy could stop and pick up any survivors. They had to keep going on in a straight path. What they call our escorts, destroyer escorts, and they can travel at pretty high speeds, were picking up the survivors from that Attack Transport, but we couldn't.

These guys that were out there in the water. They were getting awfully discouraged because they had been in the water for about six hours or seven, something like that. They were getting pretty wary. They said, the rumor was, that some of them just gave up. They thought, well we weren't going to pick them up. They were just going to drown out there so they just took off their life jackets and went under and got it over with."[37]

When Bud was asked why the LSTs didn't pick up the men in the water, he explained:

"The escorts are bigger ships so they can shoot further and they can run faster. They are all around us like a big circle.

The LSTs were too slow. If we had stopped, we would have been sitting ducks for a submarine torpedo. The destroyer escorts could run up there and pick them up and get out of there. They could run a lot faster.

They wouldn't jeopardize a whole convoy for one ship."[38]

On the 9th, *LST 919* shot down its third Japanese plane. On this day *LST 919* unloaded at Lingayen Gulf and a Life Magazine photographer took a photo of MacArthur sitting in his jeep with *LST 919* in the background. The photo was published in Life Magazine on February 19, 1945.

George Lewis of *LST 919* recalls:

"I remember that. Because what happened was we were close to the beach. We saw the crowds coming up. But just before that, a shot rang out. It was a Japanese sniper that was in a bit of a tunnel not too far off the beach. There was kind of brush there, hedges, whatever they call them. He did hit one G.I. that was standing around. Then everybody scrambled. Everybody ducked. I was up on the bow. Someone threw a hand grenade to where he thought the shot came from. Blew it up. I guess there was one single Jap in there. And along came, a few moments later, a bulldozer came and covered the hole up. That was the end of it. Everybody went back to work.

And then here comes MacArthur, maybe 15 or 20 minutes later. When he walked ashore, he got his trousers all wet. He got in the jeep and the jeep stalled. They couldn't get it started. So he sat there in front of us waiting for Army personnel to bring up another jeep. And then he got in the other jeep and they drove away. That's why he was sitting there. Normally, he would have been moved on. But he was sitting there waiting for another jeep and that's when that Life photographer took that picture.

The fighting was going on further inland. We could occasionally hear some shells going off. There was nothing on the beach, just one lone guy down in a tunnel somewhere. And they covered him up."[39]

When the *LST 919* was beached at Leyte, one of its sailors found an injured monkey on the beach. The monkey had lost its left front arm and most of his tail. The sailor brought the monkey back to the ship, cleaned and bandaged his wounds, and fed him. The monkey took a liking to another sailor, Woodrow Hinote. George Lewis would see Hinote carrying and feeding the monkey and assumed it was Hinote's monkey.[40]

One dark, moonless, overcast night, when *LST 919* was in a convoy heading back to New Guinea, George was going up to the wheelhouse to begin his watch on the annunciator. It was around midnight and as he felt his way up the ladder, he paused for a moment and looked out at the sea. Out of nowhere, something jumped on his neck and shoulders. Frightened, George screamed, reached back and

Crew of LST 919 in 1945. Mel Smith, 1st row of sailors on right; George Lewis, 1st row of sailors, 4th from right; Bud York, 4th row of sailors on left. Source: LST Home Port website.

grabbed it, and threw it over his head as hard as he could. And then he realized he had just thrown the monkey over the side of the ship.[41]

When other sailors asked about the monkey, George kept quiet. George was 18 years old; 5 feet, 2 inches tall; and weighed 110 pounds. Hinote was a few years older, much taller and weighed in at about 200 pounds.

"I was so afraid to tell anyone that I threw the monkey overboard," George explains. "My fear was, if word got back to Hinote of what I did, one dark night I would be going over the side to join the monkey."[42]

George kept this secret for almost fifty years until he saw Hinote at *LST 919*'s first reunion. As he confessed his story to Hinote, Hinote grinned and then started laughing. That night, George found out that it was not Hinote's monkey, but another shipmate's, Edward (Breezy) Carrol. Breezy has never been to an LST reunion. But if he ever attends, George is prepared to make the same confession all over again.[43]

The Japanese surrendered on August 14, 1945.

Bud York will tell you that "he was one happy merchant. There was rumors going around all the time that the war was over. It was just guys just trying to spread stuff. So you didn't know whether to believe it or not.

We were waiting to load up to go to the main invasion of Japan. We were just waiting on orders. So when they said, hey the war's over, the war's over, well, you heard that all the time. A guy said, 'No, I'm not kidding. Go up topside and see the flares and stuff going off.'

Well, when we were under an air raid, they would shoot up three red flares. When we saw that, we had to get to our gun stations. But these red flares were just going off everywhere. We didn't have any indication of an air raid. I remember seeing all that and looking at it and I thought this has got to be true. This has got to be the end of the war. There were lights coming on. The ships had their running lights on. We were not allowed to show any lights at night. So I thought this has got to be true. This has got to be it. And I was one proud guy, I'll tell you that.

There's one thing about it. People can condemn Harry Truman for dropping them atomic bombs. And it did kill a lot of Japanese people. But it would have been a drop in the bucket of what would have happened. I mean it would have wiped out probably 75 percent of the troops and the servicemen that were over there. And they would have fought to the last woman and child. Because they were that dedicated to that war."[44]

Although the war was over, *LST 919* continued to perform occupation duty- transporting troops and equipment, a medical unit, and Japanese prisoners of war. Soon after leaving Jinsen, Korea on September 30th, it was hit by a typhoon. Mel Smith described what it was like to go though these storms:

"... when I served aboard the *LST 919* and we went through some of the worst storms that mother nature threw at us, I couldn't help but marvel how well those vessels held up, the punishment those pounding mountainous waves delivered to those noble ships was unbelievable. Can you picture a flat bottomed ship for most of its 328 foot length, riding a 40 foot wave until about one-third of that length was riding clear of water on a crest of a huge wave, then crashing down into the trough, suddenly the twin screws clearing the water and attaining the speed exceeding the governor controlling the engine's R.P.M. set at 844 R.P.M.?

I stood watch in the main engine room where there were two V12 electromotive diesel engines providing the power to push that 328 foot, 50 foot beam LST at a maximum speed of 10.8 knots. The governor shut the engines down when the R.P.M. exceeded 844 R.P.M., at which time we had to manually reset the governor before the engine could be restarted.

We experienced such a storm off Okinawa in 1945. For two days we rode out that storm. We lost our Gyro compass' service, no sun to shoot, nor stars to shoot to get our position. We only prayed that we hit no other ship floundering out there in that vast sea of angry mountainous waves. I've heard of other ships ... breaking up in the storm but the LST held and brought us through. I've so often silently thanked those wonderful, dedicated workers, especially the welders for the great job they performed in building them."[45]

Mary Rossetti Fisher with Ron Adams' writing class at Broadmeadows School, June 2001. Courtesy of: Mary Fisher.

Mel has also attended his ship reunions and says:

"Our ship's crew reunions have been memorable the past few years as we get together and swap sea stories that never grow old and a few white lies I'm sure. But I don't remember having that much fun as those ole salts tell it was."[46]

* * * * *

Today, Fran Fisher Catrabone and Mary Rossetti Fisher have asbestosis, believed to be a result of working below deck on the ships. Despite this, they would do it all over again. Fran loved to weld. "We loved our work," Mary explained, "Yes, we did, we loved it. When the war came to an end and we had to leave, the women didn't want to leave."[47]

Fran sent the author a copy of the following farewell poem, written by Nancy Eaton and Mollie who were guards at the shipyard.

My People

They are taking you out of the shipyard,
Taken out singly and taken in pairs,
Perhaps it will help at your leaving
To know that somebody cares.

Someone is glad that they met you
Has a twinge in their hearts as you go,
Though our paths do not pass in the years that may come,
In my heart I think I will know,
That the friendships that we formed at Beth Hingham
With folks of all types, from all classes and climes
Have molded a more liberal outlook,
And helped us to meet anytime
That we shall encounter as we travel through life,
When the yard is a thing of the past,
For the kindred spirit ignited at Hingham,
Is a spark that forever will last.

So "Good-bye" and "Good Luck" to you each one and all
My people of the yard,
In performance of my duties have never found it hard,
To see your very viewpoint,
Hear your stories, enjoy your fun,
Now I feel I've gained your friendship, tho the yard is almost done,
You knew that, when an order was given,
I felt I was being fair,
For you knew it was my duty,
And I'd play it on the square,
And I feel that in the future as in days that have gone by,
I'll be proud of Hingham "Common" people,
Even as you and I,

Yes I worked among "my people",
Not so very long ago,
On the boats down on the wet slips,
And I'd like to have you know,
That its been my sincere pleasure
To rub elbows with the throng
Massed to-gether for one purpose
Just to help the cause along,
Common people you have heard,
Is the shipyard workers call,
But what does life consist of,
But the common things after all.

Chapter Seven

The Prairie Shipyard

"Thank All Mighty God for the lady welders of LST shipyards in WWII." - Hike Nedeff, *LST 610/325*

Mabel Ward's family moved to Utica, Illinois after the depression, her father looking for work. Mabel moved to San Diego to be with her husband, who was in the Marines. When he was shipped out in 1943, Mabel and her baby boy, Jerry, moved back to Utica and lived with her parents.

Mabel was 18 when her Dad, her sister, and she began working at the Seneca shipyard. Since her sister was only 16, she worked in the cafeteria. Her father put insulation on the inside of the LST's hull. Mabel became a welder. Mabel recalls:

"We worked nights to make five cents more per hour. We'd go to work in the evening and work all night. Eight hours, sometimes 10 hours. We started at 7 o'clock in the evening, before dark. They had these huge big lights in the shipyard on poles. We worked many times on Saturdays, as well. When we were in full swing, when they were really pushing."

Mabel went to welding school for two weeks. "It's so difficult whenever you start to weld. You have to hold that welding rod just a fraction from the metal. Because if you get too close it will stick and you have to stop and pull it loose. I would get so aggravated with this and myself that I couldn't hold it just the right distance. And I'd take my helmet off and go stand outside my booth and think of my husband in the Marines, fighting. It would give me the strength and determination to go on."[1]

Mabel remembers her helper, Ernie. "He was my helper during the whole time. He had to pull these big cables from one end of that LST to the other for me to weld. And he would set up the ladders on the outside of the ship. We would weld these anchor pads. I don't know if they weigh 8 or 12 pounds. Heavy steel. He would have to hold that up for me while I laid a bead down and he would take a slag hammer and knock the slag. And then I would put my helmet down and weld it.

This man, the reason I remember him so well, I was 18 at the time and he was 40. And I thought he was an old man! He would come to work every evening. He was not married. They teased him a lot because the lady at the boarding house where he stayed was not married either. But he would come to work and he would have tobacco juice running down the corner of his mouth. And he would be smelling like the local bar because they would all go by and have a little drink before they would come to work. However, he never, ever got out of line in any way.

We would also put curb plates on. Almost like a baseboard all along the side of that big ship. Because inside that baseboard is where they put wiring."[2]

Mabel's mother helped take care of Mabel's boy, Jerry. "I was at home in the morning and would feed him. He would play and she would watch him while I slept."[3]

There is a song that Mabel heard at the shipyard that is special to her.

"I can remember walking down those long halls with these huge lights on poles. I had never seen those tall lights. Of course, they have them everywhere now. They also had big loudspeakers where they played music. And one of the songs that came out during that time was "Have I Told You Lately That I Love You". I love it. I sort of adopted that song. I would go down that aisle listening to that music. And after all these years, every time I hear it I think of that. My daughter recently sent me a tape that she had made where she works. She recorded it because she remembers me hearing that song and claiming it was my song because I thought of my husband."[4]

Mabel would receive letters from her husband almost every day. She had no time for social events. "I didn't even go to church at that time. I had to go to work constantly and go home and play with my little boy or help feed him."[5]

Mabel's husband came back from the Pacific before the war ended. He was stationed in the Carolinas so she took their son and moved to be with her husband. She left the shipyard before it closed.

Chicago Bridge and Iron Company owned two hundred acres along the Illinois River in Seneca. In 1942, the company constructed the shipyard and 157 LSTs were built there. Its first LST, *LST 197*, was launched on December 13, 1942. Ten million pounds of welding rod were used to build these ships.[6]

Laura Heuer started working at the shipyard in 1944 as a welder's helper. Laura's welder worked near where Mabel Ward worked and Laura and Mabel became friends.

When Laura started working, she was living in Princeton, Illinois with her mother and brother. Her mother was divorced and didn't have a job. Laura's job at the shipyard made it possible for her to take care of her mother. "I took care of the rent and all. I was glad I could"[7]

In the beginning, Laura got a ride to the shipyard. "I was the seventh rider. She (the driver) had a regular car and it was full. I was so lightweight. I was skinny. I had to sit on somebody's lap every time."

Later Laura rented a room in a house that was about a mile from the shipyard. She would then walk to work.[8]

Laura recalls:

"I was a welder's helper. I helped one welder. Sometimes I had to help another welder, a German welder. He was something else. My sister was supposed to help him but she was a wanderer. She was off the boat a lot. But he would ask her to come help him with something. When she wouldn't answer his call, I would go and see what he wanted. To save her.

In the winter time, those boats were cold. They were practically a shell, a shell of a boat. They had the roof and the flooring and the wall but they were all iron. It was hard to keep warm. I had to sit a lot. I had to sit right there so I could hear my welder. If he wanted something. If he wants a machine up on top of the deck. If he wants welding rods. I had to go get them. If he wants the hose moved somewhere else.

The man I was helping, he was nice. He helped me with the hoses for the top. We'd have to bring them down from the top and down all over the place, through the port holes. Those port holes weren't very big.

I remember one night in the winter time, to keep warm, I gathered up all the lights that the welders use. A lot of the welders just let them lay. And I just gathered a lot of them up and lit them all around me. I sat right in the middle of them to try to keep warm.

I liked it there. I was one of the last ones that left. They laid all the helpers off except me and all the welders except two welders. My welder and then that German welder. So I had to help two. That was after V-Day. I stayed for awhile."[9]

Laura also didn't go out after work. "I just went back to the house. I was tired."[10]

Laura was one of the few women who was on an LST after it was launched.

"I remember one time, one of these boats had to come back because it got wrecked on the Mississippi River. It was my welder who had to repair it. It was all finished inside and everything. And it had sailors on board.

So my welder and I had to go on that boat. He had to go over the side of it and stand on a ramp down there in the water. He told me to stay up at the top there. I just took a rope and whatever he wanted sent down, put things in a pail. I tied a rope on the pail handle. Material, whatever he needed. Sent it down that way.

But I thought that at the time, women weren't allowed on the ships. They gave us a tour of it. It was so beautiful inside. That was the first time I'd seen one all finished. Nobody said anything. I was right on top there waiting to see whatever my welder was wanting."[11]

Laura met her husband after they closed the shipyard. They married in 1949 and had three children. Laura and Mabel still keep in touch.

* * * * *

Vernon Beard was a Yeoman 2/C on *LST 642*. His ship took the Marines to Iwo Jima. Vernon typed up all the movements of the day they were sent to Washington, D.C. One time, *LST 642* was anchored near Vernon's brother's ship so the two brothers were able to visit for a few hours. Vernon's brother-in-law was on the second USS *Hornet* and would later tease Vernon, calling the LST a "mud scow."[12]

A relative of Betty Rankin was an electrician at the Seneca shipyard. He told Betty that the shipyard needed workers. Betty became a tack

LST 642. Courtesy of: Ella Beard.

welder in 1943 on the day shift and worked at the shipyard for two years. She lived in Morris, Illinois, about 15 miles from Seneca, and car pooled to work with five others. Betty recalls:

"It was a wonderful experience. It was hard work. The days were long. Sometimes we worked seven days a week. You didn't have much time for a social life, that was for sure. You were too tired when you got home. By the time you cleaned up and ate, it was time to go to bed. But I enjoyed every bit of it."[13]

Betty remembers when Cesar Romero visited the shipyard. "I remember him being there. That was really the highlight, as far as seeing anyone."[14]

Cesar Romero was in his mid-thirties when he joined the U.S. Coast Guard during World War II. By the time he enlisted, he had already acted in several movies and played the Cisco Kid in a Western series. In addition to being a public spokesman, encouraging defense workers to keep their production high, he became a Chief Boatswain's Mate and served aboard the USS *Cavalier,* an Attack Transport.

Betty also attended several LST launchings. "That was a great day," she will tell you, "when one was built and ready to go."[15]

* * * * *

L.F. Grove was on *LST 607* and at the Okinawa invasion. In a letter to Russ Kopplow, he writes:

"We were in air raids every night at Okinawa. I watched the Japanese bombers cross over us. I could see them because of the powerful spotlights on the island had them lit up in their cross beams.

We had a smoke machine on the after deck. All the LST's were circled around the troop ships and they all put out a solid cloud of smoke to cover them up and hide them for protection. The smoke got so dense you couldn't see and you had to feel your way around the main deck.

The bombers would sink one or two of our ships every night in Buckner's Bay. We were anchored on the other side of the island at Otaree."[16]

After the war, Chicago Bridge and Iron Company closed the shipyard and returned to bridge construction.

Chapter Eight

Never Late for an Invasion

"You hear all this talk about the LSTs being slow. But we were never late for invasion." - Dewey Taylor to C. Ray Hall of the Louisville, Kentucky The Courier Journal.[1]

Ruie Johnson would pass Nello Golden's house on the way to school. Sometimes she would see Nello. She didn't give it much thought. After all, she was 10 years old and Nello was only 5. Ruie would never have believed it if someone had told her then that she would marry Nello one day.[2]

Ruie lived on a farm in Hardin County, Kentucky. She was the second of 14 children. Her family raised tobacco and corn and cane used to make sorghum. They lived on the money they made selling tobacco. The family then moved to Edmonson County. In 1935, her parents moved to Evansville, Indiana and Ruie went to Bloomington. She worked in a restaurant in Bloomington for two years and then moved to Evansville, Indiana.[3]

When Ruie came to Evansville, her sister had been married to Nello Golden's brother for about four years. Nello was staying with them. A few days after Ruie arrived in Evansville, Nello asked her to a show. She said yes and they started dating. They married on May 14, 1938.[4]

Ruie and Nello rented a house that was within walking distance of the land along the Ohio River that would become a new shipyard.

Evansville Shipyard, May 22, 1943. Collection of the Evansville Museum of Arts, History, and Science.

Walter Koch, of International Steel, convinced the Navy Bureau of Ships that Evansville was a good place for a shipyard. In January 1942, Evansville was selected. A joint venture, led by Missouri Valley Bridge and Iron Co. was formed to build the ships. Other members of the "Joint Venturers" included Winston Brothers, Co; C.F. Haglin and Sons, Inc.; Sollitt Construction Company, Inc; Bechtel-McCone Corp.; W.A. Bechtel Co.; and H.C. Price Co.[5]

The Evansville shipyard was still under construction when the first keel needed to be laid. So it was laid at the facilities of International Steel, a subcontractor. On June 25th, this keel, which was for *LST 157,* was moved from International Steel to the shipyard.[6] *LST 157* was launched on October 31, 1942. Evansville produced 171 LSTs.

Nello went off to the Army. A friend of the Golden family asked Ruie to go with her to the shipyard. Ruie explained, "I said I didn't know anything about welding. She said go out to welding school and learn." So Ruie did. She was in school for 2 weeks and then Ruie and six other women, including her new friend, Grace Williams, were put out on production on Skid 3. Ruie worked the third shift, from 11:30 PM to 7:30 AM.[7]

"I was there when the first ship was launched. Everybody quit working and went to the launch. Everybody on that shift and everybody off that shift were allowed to come in. That shipyard was full of people. We went in around 11:00 AM that day."[8]

Housing was short in Evansville so Ruie subrented her house. "I rented one of the rooms out to two old ladies, and I rented the upstairs out to my sister and her husband and her little girl. Grace (Ruie's friend) and I lived in the other two rooms. We had one bath, it was upstairs, and we lived downstairs."[9]

"Housing was so scarce then. People rented rooms to sleep in in shifts. One would have it for eight hours and another one would have it for eight hours and another one would have it for eight hours."[10]

Ruie walked to work but one night, when she went out, she saw a car coming up the street. It looked like the car of the man she knew that lived down the street. "So I just flagged him down and he stopped and I got in. He said, 'where are you going?' and I looked at him and it was a stranger. I said I'm going to work and he said, 'where do you work?' and I told him. He took me straight to work. When I got out he said, 'Young lady, be careful who you get in the car with now.'"[11]

Ruie and Grace occasionally went to dances. "We really worked hard. I guess we felt like we were fighting the war. We had very little time for pleasure. We worked the third shift. By the time we got off, everything that was partying was closed. We went to the Troc for dancing and the Commando in Henderson but most of the time the songs didn't start until 8 PM. We didn't have much time because by the time we got dressed to go somewhere, we had to be home to get dressed to go to work at 11:30.

I remember one time I went out there and I can't remember the name of the band that was there. I danced with several different people out there and I told some of them I guess I was a good dancer. I never had to wait for someone to dance with me."[12]

Ruie's main foreman was Fred Dixon. Everyone called him Dick. "I remember one time the main foreman fell through the skids. He fell straddling one of those skids. He fell on it. I said, Oh, did that hurt you Dick? And he said, no, it hurt my knee. He laughed. But I didn't say no more."[13]

There were a lot of soldiers in Evansville and one night Ruie and Grace went out to dinner at the Spaghetti Bowl. There were two soldiers outside and Grace asked them to come in and eat with them. "So they went in and sat down to eat and when we got done eating, one of them offered to pay. Grace said no, no, I'm paying for this. I invited you in to dinner. We sat there and talked awhile. And the other serviceman, he said, it's a good thing you paid today, he doesn't have a dime."[14]

Ruie celebrated her 33rd birthday by having breakfast in a restaurant in Owensboro, Kentucky. "There were about 10 of us having breakfast there. This boy, Pat Fitzgerald, he and his wife were along, said something about me being 33 years old. That was old back then. He said, '33 years old.' I said, don't worry, I'll be living at 83. So I forgot all about it and I hadn't seen him in years and his first wife had died and he was married again. My phone rang on my 83rd birthday. I answered it and it was Pat Fitzgerald. He said do you remember when you were 33 years old, us being in Owensboro having breakfast? I said, did you remember Pat? And he said, yes."[15] When Ruie related this story to the author, she was 92 years old.

Two months before the shipyard closed, Ruie was transferred to the ways. She was there when they launched the last ship. "A long tow. They transferred it to steel posts first, and then they laid all the plat-

Ruie Golden, Grace Williams, and Lucille Ash. September 27, 1943. Collection of the Evansville Museum of Arts, History, and Science.

forms. It went on the runways. So they turned it down on the runways. That was really hard work ... I mean climbing. Most of it was overhead work." Ruie was one of the last women welders to leave the Evansville yard.[16]

A shipyard photographer took a picture of Ruie, Grace, and Lucille Ashe one evening. Harold Gourley included the photo in his book "*Shipyard Work Force*." When *LST 325* visited Evansville in July of 2003, Channel 7 and Rich Davis, of the Courier and Press, contacted Ruie. "I never ever thought anything like this would happen. When they made my picture in the shipyard that night, that man came around taking pictures. I don't know whose pictures were made but he called me and two other girls up there and he said hold your hood in your hands. I thought that would be the end of it. Later on they put out this book, this shipyard book.[17]

When the ship was in here, Channel 7 came out and took me down to the boat. They had my picture in the paper. My pastor calls me a celebrity. One night at church he said, 'well, I'm going to ask our celebrity to dismiss us tonight.'"[18]

Lloyd Pace served as a signalman in the U.S. Coast Guard on *LST 170*. The sailor's named her the "Green Dragon." Lloyd describes the ship when they boarded her in Evansville.

"When we picked up our *170* in Evansville, Indiana, she was somewhat naked, above deck. We had to pick up our mast, rear deck gun, stern anchor, and all of our communication equipment, later on down the Mississippi and in Florida and Cuba. All below decks were ready. All other guns were in Cuba.

When we arrived in Vicksburg, we had to be "degaussed." That was a complete grounding of all of our metal parts, by wrapping the ship with neutralizing cables. Static electricity is picked up on shore and is deadly when fuel oil, ammo, etc. is used."[19]

Lloyd recalls beaching on the Island of Bora-Bora on their way from the Panama Canal to Brisbane, Australia. The trip took over three weeks.

"After we beached, and the "Pilot" from the base had left our ship, a large bunch of service guys and locals came to our bow door-ramp and wondered what our LST was, how it worked, and where we were going. With proper clearance from the "Beach/Base" authorities, we took the group on a ship tour. We showed them everything except where we were headed. They had "chow" with us at noon and really pigged out.

They thought our "two-decker" crew bunks were really great. They couldn't imagine how hot they could get when the outside temperature was 95 degrees. No Air Conditioning!!

LST 170 prepares to unload at Sansapor, New Guinea. Collection of the Evansville Museum of Arts, History, and Science.

The troop quarters were even hotter but our cooks' chow made up for a lot of things. Two cooks and two mess clerks for 120 men. When we picked up troops to take forward for an assault landing, they would have as many as 100 extra mouths to feed. We'd always load the troops with extra snacks in canvas sacks. They told us about how good they tasted, when we picked some of them up a few weeks later (mostly wounded ones)."[20]

Lloyd served on *LST 170* for eighteen months and during the time he served, it was "only hurt once by a medium bomb, dropped by a "Betty-medium bomber" which flew low under the shore radar. It came low over the trees where we were on the beach unloading some marines and their equipment. The bomb missed hitting us in a vital spot, and hurt several guys, but no one was killed. The plane didn't make it back."[21]

* * * * *

Pauline Hight's husband was a carpenter and was sent to various locations throughout the U.S. to build Army Barracks. When they finally returned to Evansville, Pauline's home town, Pauline went to Mechanical Arts School, a vocational school, to learn how to weld. Pauline remembers a terrible day she had at the school.

"We had an instructor that stayed right close by. Each one of us had a booth that we worked in. I had long hair. I wouldn't give it up. I think some of it crept from under my scarf. I didn't have my helmet on well and my hair caught on fire. The instructor came running and he caught me and he put it out. But I'll tell you what, I've never been so scared in my life. When I was a kid, I caught fire and my mom and uncle put me out."[22]

Pauline worked the graveyard shift. She had a little boy, Joe, who was two years old. She would get home after her shift, feed her son and then take him to St. Vincent's nursery. Then she would get some sleep.

"One time I made the mistake of just locking the trailer door. We had a trailer. And I locked the door and gave him a little book to look at. I was just going to take a nap. I woke up, the door was open, and Joe was no where to be found. I took off running. And I caught him, almost to school. With that baby book under his arm. I said, where do you think you're going boy? He said, 'cool.'"[23]

"The thing that I wanted to do more than anything else but I couldn't do it, because I wasn't old enough and I had a baby, was to join the Army. And the guy said, 'you have a baby here and you're not old enough anyway. And if we did take you, who would take care of your baby?' I said, his daddy. He said, 'And why isn't his daddy in service.' I said, he's doing war work but he's too old for the Army. I thought that guy would crack up."[24]

Evansville Shipyard from Reitz Hill, January 6, 1943. Collection of the Evansville Museum of Arts, History, and Science.

Pauline will also tell you about a time at the shipyard when she was badly frightened. "They sent me down in the hold of the ship to get the welding rods. I guess I got scared because I forgot how I got down there. I went down a ladder. But I couldn't find my way out. I was looking for a door. By the time I found my way and got back up top, I told them they needed to put me a door down there or bring my welding rods to me."[25]

Pauline did enjoy the time she worked at the shipyard. But, like others who worked there, she will tell you it was cold. Occasionally, when it was really cold, Pauline confesses, "Sometimes we could get together and you know, they say "abandon ship." We'd go to a little bar, dance and have fun. That was the only relaxation we got. I never got caught at it. Thank God. My old man, he didn't work there, he worked in another place."[26]

In July 2003, *LST 325* visited Evansville. "It's been my dream to go back and visit these old ships. Well, there weren't any left in Evansville. These sailors, they got together and they found one in Greece. In not too bad of shape. That's the one they brought back over here from Greece. While I was in Evansville in July for a family reunion, the old ship was on tour along with the sailors that brought it in. So you know, I had to go. I had to go on tour. I never enjoyed anything so much in my life as I did that."[27]

In June of 1944, Pauline took leave because she was pregnant. She had a baby in September 1944. After she left the shipyard, she "didn't have a chance to do any more war work."[28]

* * * * *

On May 21, 1944, the Northern Attack Force LSTs were moored in West Loch, Pearl Harbor. They were getting ready for the invasion of Saipan, their part in "Operation Forager." There were 34 LSTs moored in seven tares. *LST 353* had aboard a mortar laden LCT. The previous night, during a rehearsal, a mortar laden LCT broke loose from *LST 485*, rolled into the sea, was rammed by the next LST in the column, and sank. There were Marines sleeping in the LCT when it rolled off. It sank with a total of nineteen dead or missing and five injured men.[29]

This was the second of three mortar laden LCTs that sank. It was decided that the excess weight of the mortars and ammunition had contributed to them sinking. An order was given to *LST 353* to off load the LCT's 4.2" mortars and their ammunition. In the morning of May 21st, a working group of army men from the 29th Chemical Company, Schofield Barracks, Oahu began hand moving the mortar ammunition from the LCT into the bed of a truck parked immediately in front of the LCT on the LST's elevator. After a truck was loaded, the elevator took it down to the LST's tank deck. From there, it moved to the bow ramp and was carried to shore by an LCM (Landing Craft, Mechanized).[30]

Shortly after 3:00 PM, an explosion occurred on *LST 353*. The explosion detonated the other ammunition aboard and fire spread to adjacent ships laden with ammunition, causing more explosions. Navy and Coast Guard tugs and fireboats fought the fires and small craft rescued the men in the water. The explosions resulted in the loss of *LST 353* (built at Charleston Navy Yard), *LST 179* (built at Evansville), *LST 43* (built at Dravo, Neville Island), *LST 480* (built at Kaiser, Richmond), *LST 39* (built at Dravo, Neville Island), and *LST 69* (built at Jeffersonville). The tragedy killed 163 men and injured 396.[31]

King Richeson, a Lieutenant (jg) on *LST 179* recalled:

"We were getting ready to go to Tinian. That Sunday afternoon, we had torn the propeller off the ship and we were supposed to go in dry dock and get it fixed. The officer of the day had gone over to call the captain to let him know we were to get under way. I was the only officer that happened to be aboard at the time. That's when the explosion started. It started on the ship next to us. Almost immediately, the canvas we had on the trucks and things on the deck were on fire."[32]

Had the explosion occurred 20 minutes later, *LST 179* would have been on its way to dry dock, clear of the area.

King was in the Officer's Wardroom, censoring mail, when the first explosion occurred. He went into the passageway leading to the starboard side of the main deck and the second explosion occurred. King spent most of his time directing the injured, who were in bunks in the officer's quarter, to the stern of the ship so they could be put on LCVPs. He and the Chief Boatswain's Mate were putting a line on an injured man to lower him over the stern when the *179's* ammunition exploded beneath them. The next explosion threw King overboard.[33]

King was in the water about 15 minutes when he was picked up by an LCVP. Most of his time in the water was spent swimming under water to avoid the falling shrapnel and other debris. When the LCVP dropped King off at the Ammunition Dock, he saw his LST clouded with smoke and fires racing aft. He was put in a jeep and taken away and never saw the *179* again. King returned to the Mainland and was assigned to the USS *Alcyone*. Later he served on *LST 889*.[34]

Carlyle Harmer was also on *LST 179* that day. He was 18 years old. "When the first loud explosion happened, I was two decks below unloading cots for the Marines to sleep on. The blast knocked me up against a bulkhead and knocked me out cold.

There was another explosion and I tried to get to my feet and I discovered that I had a real bad nose bleed and a terrible headache from the concussions. I struggled to my feet and made my way back to the main deck and looked at the bow. It was totally engulfed in flames.

There was one explosion after another and someone said 'Abandon Ship, it cannot be saved.' I jumped off the ship and into the water with dozens of others heading for the shore about four hundred feet away. Red hot pieces of steel were landing in the water all around us. There were large pools of burning oil and wounded screaming men dying everywhere. To tell the truth, it was a living hell and I don't know how I lived through it. I was almost killed.

I made it to the shore and I ran up about a mile and a half to a road that the Seabees were building. A Seabee was backing up to dump a load of dirt and he yelled to get into the truck. He took a bunch of us to his Seabee base.

I went into an empty barracks and laid down in a bunk and immediately passed out from fright, pain, and exhaustion. I was in and out of consciousness for two days and nights. A friend woke me up and asked if I had eaten and I told him I was too sick and nauseated.

He got me some Seabee green clothes and shoes to wear. Then he got a couple more buddies to help me walk to a small sick bay to see a doctor and he (the doctor) said, 'what the hell happened to you.' I told him that I had been on the ship that blew up and sank. The doctor told me that I should get the Purple Heart for my experience. He gave me some pills for the headache, nausea, and pain and said to come back in a few days. We went back to the barracks and I ate some fruit and laid down on the bunk.

A few days later I had new clothes and a sea bag. They put fourteen of us on the Battleship *California.* We spent six days on the *California* and ended up at Kawajelein Island. From there we boarded *LST 477* on June 9, 1944. We immediately set sail for landings on Guam, Tinian, and Saipan in the Marianas."[35]

Francis Hillibush was a 19 year old shipfitter aboard *LST 127.* He was near the bow of *LST 127*, loading ammunition when the first explosion occurred. Fran raced up the steps on the port side, dodging shrapnel as he crossed the deck. He helped hack the lines with a fire ax to cut his ship loose from its moorings.[36]

The skipper of *LST 127* tried to take it out through the channel to the main harbor, but the channel was clogged, so he took the ship in the other direction. *LST 127* became grounded on the mud flats. Occasionally, debris from explosions landed on its deck, but they were put out with water from the ship's fire hoses. A five inch shell fell on its forecastle, making a minor dent, but didn't explode. Ensign Barr threw it overboard.[37]

* * * * *

Edith Jones worked the day shift and had passed the overhead welding test. This meant that she had a lead man with her to handle the welding cord. About the third week of welding, a switchboard was being unloaded on top of the deck. A crane that ran up and down the tracks was unloading it. It's crate had not been removed and it was set on top of the deck. The switchboard got away from the workers who were uncrating it and came down about eight feet from Edith and hit her lead man in the head. It killed him. Sparks from her severed welding cord were flying around.[38] Edith was safe, but she had just witnessed one of nine deaths that occurred at the shipyard.

On another day, Edith was climbing up a ladder and just after she passed a big round jack, it fell down and hit a man. The ends of the jack were pumped up with air to hold pieces together. The man was injured, but not killed.[39]

Edith worked on the first boat that was launched with employees on it and she was on that boat when it was launched. Since the boat

LST 237 Commissioning. Officers and men with shops building employees, June 30, 1943. Collection of the Evansville Museum of Arts, History, and Science.

would be completed in the water, she and the others had to walk up the river bank after they got off the boat.[40]

Edith quit when she became pregnant with her daughter.

* * * * *

Rumors spread about the cause of the explosions at West Loch.

James T. Cobb, 1-B-25, 4th Marine Division, related that rumors flew thick and fast about the cause of the catastrophe, ranging from Japanese sabotage to a welder carelessly igniting a gasoline drum.[41]

William L. Maxam, 2-F-10, 2nd Marine Division, said that he was told that "20 mm ammunition was being loaded aboard the ship that exploded first. The elevator cables supposedly had parted and dropped the load below decks, causing the explosion. At least that was the scuttlebutt going around."[42]

Jack M. Tagler, "L" Company, 3rd Battalion, 6th Regiment, 2nd Marine Division, said that rumors were rampant at the time of the explosions and included spies, saboteurs, workmen's welding torches, carelessness in storing ammunition and Amtrac's gasoline.[43]

Luchan L. West, "K" Company, 3rd Battalion, 6th Regiment, 2nd Marine Division, heard that men were welding on the bow doors, and some sparks set off three barrels of gasoline that were for the amphibious tractors aboard.[44]

Warren L. Boch, Navy Seabees, said the scuttlebutt he heard was that a Japanese submarine sneaked through the submarine nets that guarded the entrance to Pearl Harbor and torpedoed the first LST. This started a chain reaction with several others.[45]

Otto Bohlman, Navy Advance Base, heard one officer tell another that a welder working on one of the ships had started the uncontrolled fire and explosions.[46]

Henry Johnson, crewman on *LST 244,* said he heard that carelessness while either loading or unloading ammunition on one of the LSTs caused the whole disaster.[47]

There was no question in Phil Moses' mind, who was serving on *LST 45*, that the tragedy had been caused by sabotage.[48]

Joe Drotovick, 2-F-23, 4th Marine Division on *LST 42*, said that on his way to Saipan, Tokyo Rose broadcast the tragedy of West Loch, and that an equally disastrous fate would meet the men wherever they were headed next.[49]

Carlyle Harmer, who was on *LST 179*, wrote: "The explosions suddenly started in the afternoon and some say it was caused by workers loading ammunition but I say it was caused by sabotage by some Japanese farm workers from a sugar cane farm on Ford Island. Tokyo Rose was on the radio within a short time to report this terrible event."[50]

Corporal Bill Hoover, a Marine who was in the invasion of Saipan, later wrote to the website www.kilroywashere.org the following:

"I was aboard a LST docked at Pearl Harbor waiting for orders to combat. I was listening to the radio. A female voice said " . . this is Tokyo Rose broadcasting to the Marines in the Pacific who are going out to die." She played a little stateside music, then said *" . . . a lot of you young men sitting there in Pearl Harbor will never leave Hawaii."* The next morning, a Japanese American welder aboard one of the LST's stuck his torch into a 50 gallon drum of gasoline. The result was, if my memory is correct, 3 or 4 LST's blown up and several hundred Marines and Sailors killed or wounded. It was kept quiet in the States, but was called "the second Pearl Harbor Attack."

I don't know if it was really Tokyo Rose, but someone sure as hell said they were, and had some pretty good information."[51]

In a letter dated June 29, 1944, Admiral Chester Nimitz, Commander in Chief of the U.S. Pacific Fleet and Pacific Ocean Areas wrote the following about the tragedy:

"While there is much evidence to support the fact that the explosion was initiated in the M-3 mortar shells in the truck on the elevator, there is also evidence which might lead to the opinion that the initial explosion could have been caused by gasoline vapor."[52]

"It is considered impossible to avoid nesting combat loaded vessels between the final rehearsal and departure. During this period, repairs, water proofing of equipment, and final preparation of personnel and material for assault necessitates proximity to facilities which are not available at atolls and other anchorages. It is a calculated risk that must be accepted."[53]

Ten other LSTs moored at Pearl Harbor replaced the six LSTs that were lost and *LST 205,* which was damaged. When Francis Hillibush of *LST 127* was asked about how he felt being on one of the replacement ships for the invasion, he responded:

"We knew nothing about being a replacement or even that we were going to Saipan until we were several days at sea. We were fully loaded with troops, the 2nd Marine Division, when the explosions struck at West Loch."[54]

The LSTs of the Northern Attack Force sailed from Pearl Harbor only one day behind schedule. They made that day up en route to Eniwetok Atoll and participated, on schedule, in the invasion of Saipan.[55]

* * * * *

Welders of Way #7, March 27, 1945. Collection of the Evansville Museum of Arts, History, and Science.

Not all women welders liked their work. Catherine Newman, who worked on the skids during the swing shift, did not want to continue as a welder after the war. "I applied for a job and welding was what I got. I had no choice in the matter. I needed a job to support myself. I had little burns all over me. Healing took forever."[56]

"I worked the winter and it was cold. I wore about four pairs of pants and nine pairs of socks to keep warm. I worked the "skids" which would get covered in ice and snow."[57]

Catherine loved the dances. After work, a group of the welders would go to dance at the Brown Derby in Evansville or the Trocadero. Catherine met her husband in high school but she had to wait four years for him to return from the war so they could marry.[58]

Virginia Harville lived in Old Hickory, Tennessee. Her father worked for Dupont. He felt he was not doing enough to help the war effort, although they were making nylon for parachutes.

"It really started before December 7, 1941," Virginia explains. "My father wanted a gun. Why, I don't know; he never hunted. He bought a new Remington Automatic and was very proud of it. He got up on Monday after the Japanese had bombed Pearl Harbor on Sunday, December 7, and went to the draft board to enlist. He was 40 years old, stone deaf in one ear and couldn't hear very good in the other, and had six children.

They wouldn't take him, of course. He came back home, went to his room, got his gun, and started out the front door. My Mom was having a fit; 'What are you doing?' He said, 'If I can't go to war, my gun can.' The army was glad to get his gun. They even signed a paper saying he would get it back or they would pay for it. Never did it, of course. He wouldn't have taken it anyway."[59]

In late fall of 1942, Virginia and her two girlfriends were standing on the corner waiting for the school bus. Virginia was a senior in high school. As a convoy of trucks full of troops passed them, the soldiers dropped pieces of paper with their names and addresses on them. Virginia and her friends picked up the papers.[60]

G.L. Broxton was in one of the trucks and down to his last piece of paper when he saw Virginia. He told the driver of his truck, "This is my last one. Throw it out right here. I hope that little black-headed one in the middle gets it." Virginia picked up G.L.'s address.[61]

The teenagers' bus was in the middle of the convoy. The girls got on and then stopped to buy school supplies. But when they went out of the store, they found the convoy was clogging the street. As a result, they were two hours late getting to school, walking into the middle of their history class. As punishment for being late, the history teacher told Virginia and her two friends to copy 10 pages out of their history book, 10 times.[62]

Virginia told her history teacher that she had something more important to do first. She went through the names and addresses she had collected, selected two of them, and wrote letters to the two soldiers. One of them was G.L.[63]

G.L. wrote back to Virginia and asked for her picture. Virginia sent him one of her senior portrait pictures. He wrote and asked her if he could visit her in Old Hickory during his leave in February before going home to Coffee Springs, Alabama.[64]

Since Virginia doubted her mother would allow G.L. to just show up on her doorstep, she told him to meet her at the drugstore where she worked two days a week as a soda jerk. When G.L. walked into the drugstore and spotted Virginia, he said, 'Hey Ginger,' his pet name for her.[65]

Virginia and G.L. talked and then walked to her house. Virginia's mother sent Virginia to spend the night with a girlfriend so that she could find out more about this young man interested in her daughter. G.L. slept that night at Virginia's house. A few days later, G.L. left for his home in Alabama but came back to spend the remainder of his leave with Virginia.[66]

In December 1943, G.L. was sent overseas.

Virginia's father had an uncle living in Evansville, Indiana, so he knew about the shipyard. Her father eventually went to Evansville and went to work in the shipyard. Her father found a house after a few weeks and they all moved to Evansville.[67]

Virginia will tell you that living conditions were poor in Evansville. "Little housing – people were living in garages, out buildings, and anywhere they could. I guess it was because so many people were

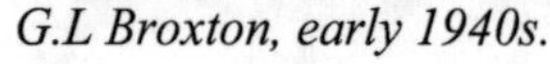

G.L Broxton, early 1940s.

Virginia Harville, early 1940s.

coming in to work in the factories and in the shipyard. My father bought us a house – a big house with 10 rooms – in an old run-down neighborhood."

The shipyard badly needed welders. I applied for a job and went to school immediately to learn how to weld. I trained for two weeks. First they put me with a ship-fitter, tacking; as the fitter cut and fitted the bulkheads, I tacked them together. A welder came later and completed the weld. This lasted another two weeks. Then I passed all the Navy tests and was on my own. Most of my welding was outside, on the hull.

This was in December. It was a very cold winter. The Ohio River froze over that winter and people actually walked across the river from Kentucky. I welded many days, sitting on ice that never melted. I will never forget the shock you get from a welding machine lead on a rainy day.

The LSTs had to be launched sideways because of the narrow river. We were allowed to stop work and watch every launching. Bands played and some distinguished person would christen the ship, breaking a bottle of champagne on the bow.

I don't remember if I worked on a certain number LST or not. They were just numbers (a lot of them!). We were very proud of our production record and of our safety record, too.

The cafeteria was a big laugh. It was so far off that one had to pack a lunch to get there! It was the same with the restrooms. By the time you went there and back, it was time to go again.

There was not a lot of time for social activities. I went to work at 8 AM. My shift was over at 4 PM. But about 3:30, someone would always come around and ask if you could work over. I usually worked four to six additional hours every night. I think the swing shift and graveyard shift had parties and dances. First shift didn't. I did go to the company picnics at Burdette Park. They were always big events and everybody enjoyed them. I know I did.

After the war, the shipyard closed; but I wouldn't have been interested in working longer anyway. You see, my fiancé was coming home from overseas and there was going to be a wedding!"[68]

G.L. made it back safely from the war. He had carried his love's photo with him throughout the war. He and Virginia were married before a judge on December 3, 1945.

* * * * *

After graduating from high school in Ziggler, Illinois, Augustine Mason moved to Evansville to live with her sister Rosie Smith, who was a riveter. Augustine went to work in the shipyard on the night

Welder, March 4, 1944. Collection of the Evansville Museum of Arts, History, and Science.

Commander Wassell and welder, April 9, 1944. Collection of the Evansville Museum of Arts, History, and Science.

shift. She did horizontal welding on the chain racks at the bottom of the ship. A few nights, she overhead welded the gun mounts on the top deck of the ship.

Augustine worked at the shipyard for several months and then decided to join her boyfriend in Oklahoma, who was in the Army. When she arrived in Oklahoma, her boyfriend had left, never telling her he was leaving.

When Augustine returned to Evansville, she decided to work in a restaurant instead of going back to her welding job at the shipyard. Augustine will tell you that she enjoyed living in Evansville during the war. Her sister would take her to the USO dances, which were right down the street from where they lived.[69]

E.J. Goodfriend was a rated Quartermaster on *LST 599* and is proud to be part of her original crew. As Quartermaster, his duties included being the Number 1 helmsman during landings or at critical times, helping with plotting courses, and helping with communications.

LST 599 was in a convoy headed for the invasion of Okinawa. Since it arrived early, it joined other ships in a natural harbor some miles away from Okinawa to await orders to proceed to Okinawa and land its cargo. E.J. describes what happened on April 3, 1945 while waiting for orders.

"During an air raid by suicide Jap planes, one of them for some reason picked *599* as a target. Even though our guns were all after it, it did slam into us. Lucky for me, our forward guns hit home and diverted the course somewhat. It appeared it was aiming for the bridge where I, among others, was in position. After being hit in a wing, the plane veered and hit midship right in the LCT on our deck. The plane went entirely through the huge piling the LCT sat on and finally stopped in a crew quarters below deck.

Had the LCT not been there, no doubt the plane would have went entirely through our hull and results would have been sea bottom for *599.*

The results were a devastating fire throughout the ship. But with help from nearby ships and our own crew, we saved the ship."[70]

Because of considerable damage, *LST 599* sailed back to the States for repair. She later served occupation duty in Japan.

E.J. will tell you, "whomever the welders were who welded the *599*, they must have been good."[71]

Chapter Nine

The Mystery Ship

The U.S. Navy wanted 300 LSTs constructed by June of 1943 and it called on the U.S. Maritime Commission to build 90 LSTs in yards already under contract to the Maritime Commission. Half of these LSTs were assigned to Kaiser Co., Inc., to be built at its yards in Vancouver, Washington and Richmond, California. Since these yards had already begun construction on Liberty Ships, Henry and Edgar Kaiser protested. As a result, a new yard was built at Richmond and was called Richmond No. 3A. It later became Richmond No. 4.[1]

Thirty LSTs were built at Kaiser, Vancouver and 15 were built at Kaiser, Richmond. In Vancouver, the first LST keel was laid down on June 15, 1942 for *LST 446* and in Richmond, the keel for *LST 476* was laid down on August 5, 1942.

The first mention of construction of the LST was in the Kaiser shipyard newspaper, *Bo's 'n's Whistle*, on September 27, 1942. It reported:

"The original shipbuilding contract at Vancouver called for the construction of 65 Liberty Ships. After the launching of two of these, however, the contract was changed and production is going forward at Vancouver on another type of vessel. Censorship restrictions forbid us to discuss it in detail here."[2]

It is interesting to note that during the last half of 1942, *Bo's 'n's Whistle* would have photos of workers at the other two Portland area shipyards owned by Kaiser but few, if any, photos of the Vancouver workers.

In the October 22, 1942 issue of *Bo's 'n's Whistle*, there is a photo of an LST with a large caption entitled "Mystery Ship." This issue reported:

"Perhaps employees of our three great shipyards have wondered why so little has been said in the *Bo's 'n's Whistle* and in the newspapers about the craft being built at the Vancouver yard. It is possible that some time in the near future censorship restrictions will be lifted so that we can tell employees of all the yards about this ingenious craft, known to Vancouver employees as the ATL Tank Landing Vessel. It is impossible to say at this time just how many of these are being built, how big they are, and how they work."[3]

In the October 15, 1942 issue of *Fore 'N'Aft*, the Kaiser Richmond shipyard newspaper, it refers to the first launching of a ship built at the 3A shipyard as Maritime Commission Number 476.

In the November 26, 1942 issue of *Bo's 'n's Whistle*, an article is entitled "Mystery Ship is Launched in 71½ Hours." It described its construction:

"Vancouver's mystery ships present engineering problems not found in the construction of a Liberty vessel. The crafts are built of much lighter plate than that used in a Liberty ship, and this necessitates more braces and stiffeners. The weight of the hull at launching is slightly less than half that of a Liberty and it contains about 180,000 feet of lineal welding ... as compared to 230,000 feet in a Liberty.

Streamlined to look at, a Navy tank lander is one of the most complicated crafts built in this area. In the outfitting phase of construction there are far more electrical work and sheet metal work than on a 10,500-ton freighter, with many intricate installations of machinery and equipment not found on other types of vessels."[4]

LST 456. Source: Bo's 'n's Whistle, October 21, 1943.

The *Bo's 'n's Whistle* finally recognizes the "Mystery Ship" as an LST in its October 21, 1943 issue where it shows photos of *LSTs 452* and *456* in New Guinea. Under the photo of *LST 456*, the caption reads: " YOU BUILT 'EM for just this moment. Here are allied forces loading on a Vancouver - built LST for the drive on Lae, New Guinea, which now serves as a base for bombing nearby Jap holdings. This ship was launched on November 18th."[5]

Alice Nenemay decided to become a welder because "it was what I chose to do and it was at a time when they needed welders to prepare more ships to send out to sea."[6] She started working at the Kaiser, Vancouver shipyard in 1942 and welded in the bottom of the ship. Alice had to go through a manhole to get to where she welded. She carried a long cord with her in order to weld.

Alice will tell you that they were not allowed to talk about the ships they built. They kept it to themselves. The workers were not told the names of ships nor where the ships were going.

Alice met her future husband at a United Service Organizations dance. He was a Petty Officer in the Navy. They married a few months after the war.

Today, Alice is a Salish Kootenai Tribe Elder on the Flathead Reservation in Montana. Alice and the other Elders meet with businesses

Kaiser, Vancouver built LSTs on Willamette River, January 26, 1943. Courtesy of: Charles Cardinell, Oregon Maritime Center and Museum. Source: Kaiser Company's Vessels Construction Program Report.

on the Reservation to help solve some of their problems. The Elders also teach their Native Language to both the young and old.[7]

LST 446 was the first LST to arrive in the South Pacific. Of the first 18 LSTs assigned to the South Pacific, six would be from Kaiser, Vancouver. Of these six, only two survived the war (*LST 446* and *LST 449*).

After *LST 179* was destroyed at West Loch, Carlyle Harmer was transferred to *LST 477* (built at Kaiser, Richmond) and participated in the invasion of Guam.

Carlyle recalls February 21, 1945: "Lt. Vinton Reinhard was showing David Barthol an IFF detonator that was in a padded metal case, lying in a foam rubber container. The officer was explaining that if the Japanese should take control of our ship that Barthol was to pull a switch and detonate the detonator. Reinhard had assumed that if the door was opened, it was safe to handle. The detonator then exploded causing the death of both men. They were buried at sea the very next day."[8]

The day continued to get worse for *LST 477*. Later that day, off Iwo Jima, Carlyle explains:

"A Japanese plane appeared on the port side and we shot it down. Then a second suicide plane appeared on our starboard side and it had a six hundred pound bomb attached and the bomb jettisoned off and landed on the main deck. It went down through the second deck, the third deck and blew a twelve foot hole in the bottom of the ship.

The plane itself went through the side of the ship and fuel from the plane and the bomb caused a terrible fire. We sat sinking in the water, the ship on fire, and no electricity, no power, no lights.

In about fifteen minutes our electricians installed jumper cables on the shattered cable wires and we got the power on and restored the lights, got both engines started, and got the pumps working and we started the fire hoses. The Marines pitched in and we got the fires out. The Marines helped man the guns and we shot down another suicide plane. We proceeded on our way to make a landing on Iwo Jima.

We had a large whole in our main deck and a huge hole in the bottom. Seven crew men were killed as were seven Marines. We saved our ship, saved the crew, saved the tanks, saved the Marines. We saved the trucks and all of our supplies and ammunitions.

All of this was hot, exciting action and we were awarded the United States Naval Commendation citation and some Purple Hearts and silver and bronze medals.

On February 23rd, we steamed on the beaches at Hot Rocks, Iwo Jima at the foot of Mt. Suribachi. We unloaded our cargo and men and supplies all the while we were getting shelled from the island and it was landing all around us.

After we unloaded our cargo tanks and men, we moved out to the middle of the bay and anchored. I was watching the big fight on the island through a long glass and I saw the flag being raised on Mt. Suribachi. It was the greatest thrill of my life.

It took thirty seven days to secure the island. We took very few Japanese prisoners because they preferred to die fighting to their death."[9]

LST 477 sailed to Guam and was put into dry dock for repairs. It then sailed to San Diego. It sailed back to Japan to participate in occupation duty. The ship was turned over to the Japanese. Carlyle recalls:

"On the 9th of March 1946, the remaining thirty six men of the crew stood at attention and observed the decommissioning ceremony and watched our stars and stripes come down and we gave our fighting lady the *LST 477* to the Japanese. We sadly picked up our sea bags and our belongings and left our ship for the last time. It was a very, very sad experience and one that I will never forget in this lifetime."[10]

Carlyle will also tell you:

"The time that I spent in the Navy was very action packed and thrilling. It was very scary to stand on the deck of a burning ship that is blowing up and sinking and dead bodies all around you. All the time you are firing your gun at suicide planes. It is an ordeal that a person will never forget. I had dreams and nightmares for years. But I am very proud that I could serve my country that I love so very, very much.

One day in Midland, Texas at the Confederate (nka Commemorative) Air Force building there was a Veterans Day ceremony honoring all of the Veterans. The building was packed with little kids and their parents, principals, teachers, and news media. The kids danced and sang songs and then at the end they cheered for the veterans. The noise was deafening.

They then asked the veterans to walk by the little kids and shake hands and I saw the prettiest little girl I have ever seen.

She said: "Thank You Mr. Veteran for fighting for me and saving the Country."

With the tears in my eyes, I shook her little hand. I told her that first, for you, I would do it again. First for her and all of the little kids."[11]

Chapter Ten

Other Ships/Other Trades

Henry J. Kaiser owned three shipyards in Portland, Oregon's metropolitan area. After 30 LSTs were built at Kaiser, Vancouver, the shipyard built aircraft carriers, attack troop carriers, and C4 troop transports. The Oregon Shipbuilding Corporation in Portland built Liberty and Victory ships. Kaiser, Swan Island built Fleet Oilers.

In June of 1943, E. Jean Wheeler's mother traveled from their home in Klamath Falls, Oregon to Portland to attend the birth of her grandchild, Jean's sister's first child. Jean's mother found out about the need for workers at Oregon Shipbuilding and took a job there. She convinced Jean, who was 17 and would be a senior in high school in the Fall, to join her in working there.

Jean's mother found Jean a room with an acquaintance who lived over 20 miles away in Newberg, Oregon. Jean would take the bus that went from Newberg to the shipyards in the Portland area.

Jean describes her experience in welding class. "I was able to pick up on the horizontal welding, but the vertical was a real challenge, and the overhead was downright *impossible*. Evidently no one cared too much about my skill as an overhead welder, so I was given the test to prove my competency; however it was evident that I was not too *competent* in the vertical portion of the test. After several failed attempts, the young man giving me the test felt sorry for me, and took the welding rod from my hand, and did the vertical weld for me and verified that I was now a "certified welder." It was probably a *big* decision to figure out what to do with me!"[1]

A team of ship fitters needed a welder to work with them on the deck, so Jean joined them. "My job was to weld what was known as a "dog". This dog was welded onto the deck near the seam line; then the ship fitter would slip a wedge underneath the welded dog from the opposite side on a different steel plate, hit the wedge with a sledge hammer, until they were sure the deck was level. Then I had to spot weld the steel plates into position so they would hold until a professional welder followed to finish the job.

The "good news" was that not once did one of those welded dogs fly off during the whole time I worked with the ship fitters, so I did have something to be proud of. After the deck was welded together by the professional welder, the little dogs were removed by another person using a cutting torch, that way the deck did not have a bunch of little metal pieces staggered all around, in case anyone was wondering."[2]

Jean only worked at the shipyards during her summer vacation of 1943. "I was lucky to have a day job, and during our lunch break at the shipyards, it was quite common to have one of the ships christened with a bottle of champagne, and sent down the ways. I attended several of those events in my first days as a *competent* welder. I felt I had earned the right, and even though I never ever welded again, I can truthfully say my very first job was doing my part to help win the war."[3]

Nell Conley was also a welder at Oregon Shipbuilding. Her husband went into the service and Nell had a four year old daughter. She had tried working at other places, but found that her mother, her daughter, and she could not live on $60 a month. Nell enjoyed the work.

"It was fun watching that weld bubble out of this rod we held in our hands and actually make a connection in something much, much stronger than we were. And the skill, I compared it with crocheting or knitting. You used the same kind of skill trying to make everything as neat as possible, as strong as possible while you were working on it. We took a lot of pride in doing a good job on that.

I think I had more fun doing it than lots of women because this is the Rose City and I welded a rose in each one of the fantails of each of the Liberty ships I worked on. I have been expecting, all the time since then, to be caught and actually arrested for having marred our Country's materials. But they haven't caught up with me yet."[4]

Nell remembers some of the people that Kaiser brought in from the South. One woman she remembers in particular.

"And she had, are you ready for this? All of her front teeth were gold. And of course that led to questions. Her answer was - she and her husband had run off together when she was just a young teenager. And her husband had her teeth removed and replaced with gold to show her pappy that he could take care of her. I would like to see the man that I would give up my teeth for!"[5]

Nell will tell you that the management of Kaiser tried to make the shipyard as safe as possible. Despite this, one day, as Nell was working on the outside shell of a ship, she fell off a scaffold backwards and broke an arm. She had stepped back a little too far and fell about 10 feet. She put her arm out to prevent her head from hitting the ground. Luckily, that was the only injury. Nell was back to work in a week with her arm in a cast. She would steady the stringer with her cast.[6]

After welding for a while, Nell became ill with a bad sinus infection. After being off work for quite a while to recover, someone suggested to Nell that she should become a crane operator. For the rest of the war, Nell operated a crane at the shipyard.[7]

* * * * *

Madra Hullinger left Waterloo, Iowa to work on the Fleet Oilers at Kaiser, Swan Island. Her husband was in the Army. Madra was working at a meat packing company in Iowa. She told her girlfriend, who lived in Portland, that she wasn't happy there. Her friend told Madra she could get her a job at the shipyard.

Madra took the train to Portland in 1942 to work in the office at the shipyard. She noticed that welders were getting $1.50 an hour, over twice as much as she was making at the meat packing company in Iowa. She went to welding school for five days and caught "on to the welding in nothing flat."[8]

Madra welded on the ways and the outfitting dock. She worked the graveyard shift. One day, Madra had a bad experience with one of her crew members.

"He bragged that he could date me and I said, 'Oh no, you can't.' He then grabbed my breasts and I hit him with my fists. He turned me into the Office and I was called in to tell my side of what happened. Needless to say, he was told to keep his hands and remarks OFF. He told others on the crew that I'd look pretty bad laying at the bottom of one of the tanks on the boat, so I always watched out for him."[9]

Madra liked Oregon and wanted to stay, but her husband worked at John Deere in Waterloo before joining the service. He had his job back as soon as he returned home from the war.

* * * * *

Louise graduated from high school in Pleasanton, Kansas in May 1944. Her father, brother, uncle, and several cousins were working at Kaiser, Vancouver. They got Louise a job as a welder's helper. But she wouldn't be 18 until August. "When one of my cousins went with me and told them I was born in April, they wanted to see a birth certificate. The longer the hassle, the louder he got until I think they said OK to get him out of the office. So I went to work on second shift on Way 2 as a helper on an all man crew.

Right away the guys said I should learn to weld so I'd make more money. So they gave me a few lessons on flat and vertical weld, but no overhead. You could weld if you passed either one. When I went to take the test they made me try all three and by some fluke I passed all three so I was considered a certified welder."[10]

Louise went back to Kansas in 1946 to be a bridesmaid for a cousin. She met a young man who was just home from the Navy. They started dating and married in 1947.

* * * * *

Willamette Iron and Steel was a small shipbuilder in Portland that built Transports, Mine Sweepers, and Submarine Chasers. Landing Craft, Mechanized, or LCMs, were built at Gunderson Brothers in Portland. The LCMs were 50 feet long and could carry a single tank and four to six crew members. Many were carried on the LSTs.

Mavis lived in Vader, Washington. In 1941, after graduating from high school, Mavis and her girlfriend, Georgie traveled to Portland and became shipfitter helpers at Willamette Iron and Steel. As soon as they opened a welding school, Mavis and Georgie learned to weld.

Georgie and Mavis would usually go home on the weekends, taking the bus or train. On Saturday nights, they would go to Grange dances with their friends from home.

"When we were welding on the bends, it would be out in the weather and we were glad that we had to wear leathers as it was warmer. We were always glad when we were sent to help finish in the lower parts of the ships as it was inside."[11]

In the Fall of 1941, Mavis met her husband, Mike Kyle. He was in a Texas Army unit that had been sent to Washington to guard the railroad bridges between Seattle and Portland. On November 8, 1943, they married in Timpson, Texas.

When she returned to Portland after the wedding, Mavis took a job with Gunderson Brothers. She was a stainless steel welder on the super structure of the ships.

While in Portland, Mavis lived in a boarding house in the southeast part of the city. The boarders had to give their ration books to the cooks at the boarding house.

"My girlfriend Georgie and I went to the Broadway Theater to see the movie "This is the Army." It was the fanciest theater in Portland at the time. We also ate Chinese every Sunday afternoon at the Mandarin. It was the nicest Chinese Restaurant back then too. We went out to Jantzen Beach to hear and dance to the Big Bands. The only one I can remember is Charlie Barnett. We would have to ride buses out and we came back late, so we always went in a big bunch. Much safer that way."[12]

Mavis' husband, Mike went to France on D-day and went in on an LST. He survived the war but was injured. When he came home from the war, they moved to a farm in Texas. "We lived on a farm our first 20 years and I put my welding to good use. I made my own clotheslines poles and helped when other welding needed to be done."[13]

* * * * *

Dora grew up on a farm in Idaho, one of nine children. Her mother died when she was seven and by the time she was 12, she was the oldest girl. She ran a household of six people with her father. In 1942, in Rigby, Idaho, Dora and her friend, Margaret, attended a class that taught young high school graduates basic skills. The organiza-

Dora Jockumsen on the left and Dorothy Kiggans, February 1945. Courtesy of: Dora Jockumsen

tion that sponsored the class sent Dora and Margaret by train from Pocatello, Idaho to Seattle, Washington.[14]

At first they worked for a company winding reels of wire. When Dora heard that Lake Washington Shipyard was hiring electricians to build Mine Sweepers, she got a job there as an electrician's helper. She worked there for about 18 months. She lived in Seattle and would take the ferry five days a week to the shipyard in Kirkland. The shipyard cut back on staff and Dora went to work for Boeing as a welder's helper.[15]

In 1945, Dora returned to Idaho and married Chris Jockumsen. They had met before the war in a bowling alley and spent time at the roller skating rink. During the war, Chris was in the Air Force as an electrician.

Dora will tell you that "Seattle and Kirkland, at that time, were such neat places. We rode the busses everywhere. I spent a lot of evenings at dances - met some really nice sailors. I feel that I became the person I am now because of the experience."[16]

Dorothy and Jim Kiggans, December 7, 1941. Courtesy of: Dorothy Kiggans

Dorothy also worked at the Lake Washington Shipyard and became friends with Dora. She grew up in Tennessee, the oldest of seven children.

"My boy friend and I were playing outside when my Dad called us in to listen to the "Philco" radio that the Japanese had attacked Pearl Harbor. That very night my uncle in Seattle called my Dad that there was a call out for workers in the shipyard. Dad, my brother, and boy friend left the next week to go out. When school got out, my sisters, brother and mother went out, and I went to the union office where there was a need for women electricians.

So I hired in and was trained for three weeks - the basics of Marine wiring. It was a lot different when I got on the ship the next day. I had never worn pants. I got a couple pairs of men's coveralls and wore them to work."[17]

Dorothy became a Journeyman Electrician within three months. Her boyfriend, Jim Kiggans, was a welder at the shipyard until he joined the Marines.

In 1943, Dorothy traveled by bus from Seattle to El Centro, California to see Jim before he was shipped out. "There was a transportation strike in Portland and our bus was stopped as well as city transportation. So I had a hectic, scary two days– hotels were overcrowded. My first trip anywhere alone. So I was happy to get out of Portland. I never told my folks how scared I was."[18]

When the USS *Mobjack* was ready for a trial run, Dorothy and Dora hid in a huge tool box. "After we were out in Puget Sound, we strolled out like we were supposed to be there. After the shock, the crew was very good to us - just let us work when needed - like we were suppose to be there! When the ship was commissioned, one of the Chief Petty Officers invited me and a sailor asked my friend (Dora) and it was a very exciting experience."[19]

Dorothy also went to work for Boeing after the shipyard cut back. "I was working there on B29s and was coming out of the plane when they announced Roosevelt's death. We rolled that plane out the door with a banner, "On to Tokyo." Since the Bomb was dropped from a B29, we wonder by chance if it was one we worked on."[20]

In 1945, Dorothy's family moved back to Tennessee. She was working the graveyard shift at Oak Ridge Atomic when the "news boys were screaming the news of the Atomic Bomb."[21]

The summer before the author was married in 1977, a friend and coworker said to her that there will always be someone that you didn't marry that you will forever carry in your heart with fondness. This is true for Dorothy.

"A little special about my shipyard experience. I met a Chief Petty Officer. He was so sweet to me. Wanted me to marry but here I was *almost* engaged to Jim (we dated eight years). My Dad forbade me to drop Jim. The Chief was Catholic and I'm Southern Baptist and I gave his ring back.

Well, I never heard from him (I did get letters but they weren't given to me.) Anyway, I did love Jim too and we got married and had a good life. But, I'd always wondered about the Ship *Mobjack.* If it got sunk - if the fellows made it. About three years ago, I mentioned it to my son - and he looked on the computer internet. There were two men by that name. I called the one in Idaho and got his wife. He'd only been dead a couple months and I had been there (Idaho) two or three times. I'm glad he had married."[22]

Dorothy and Jim married in 1946 and had seven wonderful children. Dorothy worked for 28 years as the Cafeteria Manager of her local school system. Throughout the years, Dorothy and Dora have kept in contact and occasionally visit each other.

Chapter Eleven

State of Life

Blossom Ann Dobson's maternal grandparents immigrated to the United States from Italy in the early 1900's. "There were eight in the family," Blossom explains, "and they were dirt poor. So I gather when my mother was young she said I'm not going to be dirt poor ... Mother wanted the "state of life." I wanted to go into nursing and get down with the common people. I couldn't do it.

So I started working at Meier and Frank (a department store in Portland, Oregon). On the 10th floor. I learned how to use a calculator. I wrote all the bills.

And the war came along and Margaret, next door, got a job down at the Swan Island shipyard."[1]

Blossom, who prefers to call herself Ann, was an only child and lived in Portland with her mother, who was divorced.

"My Aunt Rose wanted me to go into the Service because she thought I would be a good leader. Well, I told my mom I'm going to join the Service. This was when the women first came in. And she started to cry and said, 'All I've done for you and you want to join the Service.' I stopped. I was a fool. I should have gone on. But my mother had given up so much for me.

There were three of us that grew up on 48th Street. Margaret was the cute redhead. Betty was my girlfriend and then me. And so Marg was talking to my mother and said I should come down to the shipyards.

B. Ann Dobson when she was 18 years old. Courtesy of: Debbie Engel.

My mother said, that's not a "state of life" for Blossom. But it was money. Better money. So that's where I ended up."[2]

Ann began working at the Kaiser Shipyard on Swan Island in 1942. She took the bus to work.

"I wanted to work on the line. That's where they put everything together. On the line. A boat was built every three months. We had three shipyards going 24 hours a day for these ships. Every three months, they would send a boat down. That's when I got to see one.

I worked in the office. This is the deal ... when you start to build or construct a boat, you need all this, there's screws and nails and pipe and all that stuff. Well when they need it, it has to come through our office because we're the bookkeeping office. And it starts out with me. You got a big book there, you go see how much screws are, how much nails, how much pipe, how much sheets are. And then you figure it out. And you do it on the Comptometer (an early calculator).

Everything that came through down on the line, would come through me. And from there it went to Katy Gray. She would check my work. If it was wrong, it would come back to me and she would say, this is what you did wrong. There used to be numbers with little letters behind them and if you didn't look at the little letters behind the screws or the nails, then it came back to you so you did it again.

If it cleared Katy Gray, it went down to the other end of the room. Helen Corvallis had a —I don't know what it was—she put it on this roll. She hooked it up there. And then she would turn it. And it would turn all these slips of paper out for various parts of the Island. Whomever wanted it.

It was a round thing and she would hook it up here and you didn't have electricity. None of this stuff is on electricity, you understand. And then you hooked it up on top, she hooked it down and then she would turn it. She would turn all day. She would always say "I'll trade you jobs." And then from there it would go back to the boss that was the head of us and from there it goes down to the line. It was the most tiresome job."[3]

Ann and her friend, Betty, went to the USO dances. On Sundays they would catch a bus in downtown Portland that would take them out to the USO hall near the airport.

"That was our getting out, of meeting people. You would dance with the guys. I loved to dance. I was such a good talker. And when we came home, we walked down the middle of the street. She (Betty) was up at the head of 48th and I was at the bottom. And we would walk in the middle of the street and I would sing going down the middle of the street. Scared to death. I never ran because you're not suppose to run because people would run after you. So you just walked down the middle of the street. Here I am ... Here I am ... Here I go and singing and you finally got in. I don't know if anybody else did that.

Around the corner was George White (George A. White Service Men's Center). Pretty soon it got boring at the USO because they didn't have enough room. So we went down to George White. George White had two floors."[4]

Ann's first love was Bob. "I often wondered what happened to him. Betty and I used to go ice skating on Saturdays and we met him ice skating. When I went to get a date to go to my prom, and didn't have anybody, I asked him to go.

Bob was at a camp overseas. They saw the Japanese coming over and they didn't have any guns. They threw potatoes at them. All the guns and all their ammunition were up in the hills. I guess there were tunnels up in the hills. When he came home he would tell me about that.

I wrote to him. But bless my mother, she called his mother and his mother said he was married. And my mother said you don't go around with a married man and that was the end."[5]

Ann remembers having extra money from her job but she was unable to spend it because of the shortages. "We couldn't get candy, we couldn't get nylons, so what did we do? We got some kind of stuff that we put on our legs. You rub it on your legs and it makes them brown. Then you get a black pencil and go up from the middle part of your ankle, all the way up for the line. Those were nylons because we couldn't get nylons."[6]

Ann saw a photo of Al Kocher in the *Oregonian* and she had a strong feeling that he was the one she would marry. Al's brother was married to Ann's cousin. "I saw Al in the *Oregonian.* It was the first part of November. In 1945—because he had just come home. And I came in and I showed Helen Corvallis, the guy I'm going to marry.

I met him one day. We were coming home on the Foster (bus). There he was standing there. He came up to me and he said, 'Aren't you?

Alfred Kocher welcomed home from the war by family. Courtesy of: Debbie Engel.

You have a different name.' And I said my name is Ann. He said, 'no'. And I said Blossom."[7]

When the war was over, Ann was terminated from the shipyard. "That was the end of the boats. I had met Al by then. By the time that happened, you gotta remember the war was over. The men were coming home. And guess what. We had to give up our jobs. I'm sorry we didn't fight it, but these boys were overseas two, three, and four years and they couldn't call home.

And when they came home, they wanted their wife in the kitchen. And you'll talk to a lot of them our age. We're all sorry that maybe we should have kept our jobs. But they wanted us in the home and we hadn't seen them for three or four years."[8]

Ann would have continued working at the shipyard if she hadn't been terminated. "When you're working down there, you were working for a reason for our boys to come home. When we were in the shipyards, we figured we were doing something. So were those girls that were on the line. They did it. All the women worked as a team."[9]

Ann and Al married on September 12, 1946 and had four children.

Chapter Twelve

The Korean War

Although hundreds of LSTs were scrapped after World War II, many were recommissioned for the Korean War. *LST 1152*, built in Seneca, Illinois, was one of them.

Major Thomas was assigned to *LST 1122* in October 1952. "I think fate has had something to do with my assignment to the LST because when I was in high school, during study hall, I would get an encyclopedia and go through it looking at pictures and I would stop when the pictures of LSTs would appear."[1]

Major was an engine man and also responsible for all ballast control. "Any time the Captain would notice the ship not on an "Even Keel", he would locate me and say, 'Thomas, she is off a half bubble, get her leveled up.' He had up on the bridge a thing called an "Inclinometer", which would show the level. I also had one in the engine room to use as a guide when pumping ballast to level the ship. I would pump water from a side ballast tank or pump water into a side ballast tank to maintain the ballast. Some days when the Captain could not readily locate me, he would pass over the PA system, 'Thomas, she is a half bubble off' and I would know right away I would have to take care of this."[2]

"During the war, we transported many Army and Marine troops for attacks. If we picked them up at Sasebo, Japan, we would have them aboard for at least a couple of days, during which time we would become acquainted with some of them.

LST 1122 and 827, Korea, 1951.
Source: LST Home Port website.

They had living compartments between the stern and our living quarters. When we walked through the compartments, they would talk to us. We would ask them where they were from; they would ask us where we were from, etc. We took this one particular company to the east side of the peninsula for a counter attack around the Wonson area.

They had a little dog for their "mascot", which I know many of us had petted during the travel time. We hit the beach, dropped them off and not long after we had dropped them off, "Moscow Molly" announced over our radio, "Well, I see the USS *LST 1122* has just made a counter attack at Wonson, and we just wanted you sailor boys to know that the entire company, including the dog, has been killed." I will never forget the guys I had met, talked to, the dog we petted, and how terrible it still remains in my mind those words of Moscow Molly."[3]

Major was also a member of one of the LCVP boat crew. One day they had lowered the LCVP and were getting ready to make contact with friendly forces on an island. They were waiting for the officer to come aboard the LCVP. "We waited for a while when the officer that was going to man our boat waved for us to "come alongside", which we did. He gave us instructions stating that the ship had to go pick up a downed pilot immediately. The water was extremely cold so time was of the essence, along with the fact that harm could come to him if enemy forces would see him in the water.

The ship was in such a hurry that they didn't have time to take us back aboard. The time of day was about 9 AM or so in the morning. It was extremely cold already for us waiting in the peter (LCVP) boat. The instructions of the officer were to stay and wait in the same area until the ship returned ... We waited, waited, waited, and we were getting colder by the minute.

Noon time came and went, evening came and went, night fell upon us and we were still getting colder and colder as time went by. We kept looking toward the horizon and still no LST. The only way we had of keeping warm ... we took the engine cover off one side of the engine and we all huddled alongside the idling diesel engine ... We would walk around the bow of the boat trying to keep our feet and legs warm.

The next morning, just after daybreak, we finally saw a ship on the horizon, and praying it was ours ... We were in that boat for just about 24 hours without drink, food, or enough warmth. As soon as we could, we met up with the ship and they dropped us a thermos of hot coffee ... It seemed forever getting the boat up in the davits and finally getting down below to warm up ... To this day, I cannot tell when my feet are cold, hot or wet. The only way I can tell if they are cold, hot, or wet is to feel them with my hands."[4]

Major recalls another time when "We off loaded ammunition on one island, a huge stack built up during the unloading process. We pulled ourselves off the island with the stern anchor and under the ship's main engine propulsion and heard this loud "whistling" noise. A shell or bomb landed on the huge stack of ammo, a terrible shock wave, huge ball of orange fire, and black smoke. We saw several forms, like people sailing through the air above and around the explosion area. We presumed they were army or guerilla personnel being hurled around and probably blown to bits. After the smoke cleared, the pile of ammo was gone."[5]

LST 1122 participated in Operation "Big Switch", the exchange of prisoners of war. Major explains, "The plan was to build cages on our tank deck to retain the prisoners during the travel from Koje-Do to Pusan, Korea. There were ten cages built on the tank deck to hold 100 prisoners each. We loaded the sick and wounded prisoners first. The army would have lines of their personnel from the prisoner "pens" to the beach and our ship. I never could understand why they would have machine guns on both sides of the path, from the pens to the ship. I really couldn't understand why they thought the prisoners, especially the sick ones, would run. They were all on an island, very small, so where could they go?

We transported the sick and wounded first ... We were one of the first LSTs to take a load there ... When we were transferring the prisoners, the first load ... some of the higher ups forgot to figure where these people were going to go pee and poop. So they started pooping in the "elephants feet", cut outs in the deck where heavy chain hooks go for securing tanks, trucks, etc. Well, for two days travel time, those "elephants feet" filled up pretty quickly and they started going in the corners of their pens. After two days, it smelled so bad on the tank deck that we couldn't hardly stand it on the entire ship. The smell was going everywhere. So finally after getting the first load off the ship, we had to use heavy pressured fire hoses to wash the entire tank deck area.

The next trip, we loaded the ones that were not injured nor sick. They were mean as hell. They built in to each pen a sort of outdoor type potty framework with what they call a "honey bucket" under each hole. The rub came when they had to dump them each day. They had prisoners using a long pipe and the bail of the honey bucket with a pipe that ran through it to carry it topside and dump them out. Guess when they dumped them? Noontime when most of us were eating and again the smell would carry throughout the entire ship and even in the engine rooms because the engines sucked air down the access trunks into the engine rooms. What a terrible stink.

Loading the hostile prisoners was quite a traumatic time. The army personnel had long lines from the pens to the ship and machine guns about every 50 feet or so and we saw some of the prisoners break away from the line and they were shot on the spot. I think there were three that we saw break away. The reasoning for this was the prisoners knew when they were sent home and the army generals knew they surrendered, some of them would be shot by a firing squad.

The hostile prisoners were constantly trying to escape, even while aboard the ship. They would start chanting, yelling, then banging their chow trays against the sides of the ship and the pen's two by fours. They would constantly make noise, scream, so the army people would take fire hoses and turn high-pressure water on them, flipping them head over heals and just totally saturate them. The next thing they would have to do is gas them. So everyone on the ship, especially in the engine rooms, had to wear gas masks because the gas would eventually creep into the engine rooms and all over the entire ship. That would make the prisoners sick. They would quiet down, start puking all over. They would be quiet for the rest of the day because they were sick.

Then after we got the hostile prisoners unloaded, we had to again hose down the entire tank deck area to get the putrid smell to go away. I don't remember just how many trips we made hauling prisoners but it was a hell of a job.

The last few loads of prisoners we transported were "Anti Communist" and they knew they would be shot by firing squads when they were back in their own country. We would let them have full run of the ship. They loved the movies we showed every evening. They kept asking the movie projector operator to show the movie over and over. During the days, we would give them "chipping" hammers to chip paint on the main deck and if you turn loose a couple hundred prisoners banging on the main deck with chipping hammers, the noise is unbearable. One would have to go below decks and get away from all the noise. We felt somewhat sorry for those prisoners because they knew and we knew they would probably be killed when they got back."[6]

On July 1, 1955, *LST 1122* was renamed the USS *San Joaquin County*. The ship also served in the Vietnam War.

* * * * *

In 1951, Richard Arnold was recalled into the Navy and assigned to *LST 742* (built at Dravo, Neville Island). "We transported refugees from the North Korean islands to South Korea. Of course, with the OK of the North! At times they would forget and fire at us. Not while we were loading refugees but while we were afloat in some bay.

We would beach the ship and then the large tides of maybe 30 feet went out and we would be a half mile from the water. We would load

LST 742 loading vehicles at Wolmi-Do Island, Inchon Harbor, South Korea on October 13, 1950. Source: U.S. Naval Historical Center.

the refugees. They walked right on board. The tide came back in and we retracted off the beach. While we were on the beach, they could have taken us with a company of infantry. Of course, they wanted to get rid of the refugees more than attack us."[7]

On July 1, 1955, *LST 742* was renamed the USS *Dunn County*.

* * * * *

Several LSTs were converted to landing craft repair ships (ARL). *LST 962* was built in Hingham in late 1944. She sailed to the Gibbs Gas Engine Works yard in Jacksonville, Florida where she was converted to an ARL. On May 10, 1945, she was recommissioned as *Romulus* (ARL-22). Conversion included removing the bow ramp and doors and sealing the bow. Derricks, booms, and winches were added to haul damaged landing craft on board for repair.[8]

On the tank deck, from aft to forward, was a large wire cage for spare parts. Next to it was the precision metal working area. The engine rebuilding area included a large cook out tank for cooking out engine blocks. On the port side of the tank deck, across from the engine rebuilding area was the electrical workshop. The metalsmith area was in the forward area of the tank deck.[9]

A salvage diver and his helper were part of the ARL crew. The diver was also qualified in underwater cutting and welding.[10]

Russ Kopplow served on the *Romulus* for a portion of the Korean war. "*Romulus* was the only repair ship in Inchon Harbor during the prisoner exchange. There were three hospital ships there and in the heat at that time of year there were lots of burned out electric motors for our electricians to rebuild.[11]

Most of the ships had open well decks. They had chicken wire cages built on the well decks, many times full of Korean prisoners. Not a comfortable arrangement, so speed was appreciated. Our repair gangs worked 24/7 in three shifts ... All unnecessary lights and ventilation were off. The engine room temperature often hit 125-130 degrees Fahrenheit and we often traded every hour with the top side watch ... After a week, things slowed up quite a bit and repairs no longer had to work three shifts."[12]

Fortunately, the *Romulus* was never shot at even though it was in the war zone. Russ recalls his scariest incident:

"I was strolling down the starboard main deck, having just come from a B.S. session in the boiler room, when I heard this strange hissing sound. Reminded me of a pinched sheet exhaust pipe on a car. Ding! Ding! Starboard main engine running hot, restricted exhaust? Only thing, that exhaust stack was almost big enough for me to crawl through!

At the time our division had no Chief or First Class so we Petty Officer's in charge had direct access to the Engine Officer. I went and found him and presented my theory and he listened. Somehow he found a round vanity mirror and we cobbled it to a mop handle and, bingo, my theory was right - stack was half plugged.

Next step, get the deck gang and Bo's'n and rig a Bo's'n chair. Then a five foot long metal bar and bundle yours truly up in life jackets and over I went (in the middle of the Pacific). Engine was stopped and each time the ship rolled and swung me into the hull, I took a jab with the bar. I had to use my feet to keep my face from smashing into the hull and jab at the same time.

About a dozen pokes and the mass dislodged and fell into the water. It was still hot enough to hiss when it hit the water. The cause? A valve that fed salt water and sprayed into the stack started leaking and the combination of salt water and heat built up a blob big enough to half plug the stack."[13]

The crew of the *Romulus* affectionately called it the Rom Dom. One of Russ' crew mates composed the following poem sung to the tune of three men in a tub.

Rub a Dub Dub, that Romulus tub,
crossing the ocean blue.
We'll roll like a tub, singing Rub a Dub Dub,
cause our hearts are breaking in two!
Now the old Rom Dom is Number One in a line of T's you see,
a little heavier than the rest but one of the best
for sailing the seven seas.
Singing Rub a Dub Dub, oh what a tub,
your guts seem to twist and twirl.
Every time you take a roll in this flat bottom hole,
you'll swear it's the end of the world.[14]

Chapter Thirteen

Your Daughters Thank You

When the women left the shipyards, many of them would have liked to stay. But they were never given that option. However, they took with them the knowledge that they could do anything. The men who married them also knew this. So did the sailors on the LSTs who knew that women had built their ships.

And so the women welders, all the women who worked in the shipyards, their husbands, and the sailors knew that if women could build ships in World War II, then their daughters could also do anything.

I was never told by my parents that I couldn't become an engineer. They never said that girls weren't good in math or science. They knew better.

And a generation of daughters born during the baby boom knew, although it was left unspoken. They felt the strength of their mothers and the support of their fathers.

To the women who welded the LSTs, to the women who worked in the shipyards, to the sailors who sailed on the ships, and to all the women and men who worked on the home front or went to war ... Thank You ... For Saving Our Country.

Acknowledgments

I wish to thank all the women and men whose stories are told in this book.

As a result of my request that was published in Reminisce Magazine, I received several letters from women and men. Although I did not use every letter, all of them were appreciated. In addition, there were letters which led me to sources that helped me identify women who welded the LSTs. These letters were from Evelyn Nyberg, Lenora Gahn Kastner, Hazel Einfield, Dean Rider, Billy Smith, Roland Dahl, Douglas King, Roland Jennings, Charlie Wright, Leonard Johnson, Phil Barker, Lorene Sullivan, Margaret Sondey, Patty Chavez, Mary Cole, Howard Spencer, Georgia Fields, John Small, and Ernest Collins.

A thank you to Robert Pozerski who sent me the video, "Remembering the Hingham Shipyard."

Others who have helped me include Martin Cohn, Trustee of the Hingham Shipyard Historical Foundation; Thomas Lonnberg, Curator of History at the Evansville Museum of Arts, History and Science; Yvonne Knight, Administrator of the Howard Steamboat Museum; Charles Cardinell of the Oregon Maritime Museum; Bob Bridgeman of the Illinois LST Association; Darleen Mead of the *LST 534* website; David Baird from the LST Home Port website; John Cindrich, Editor of the Zajednicar; Jessica Lemieux from the Bancroft Library, UC Berkeley; Rich Davis of the Evansville Courier and Press; William Trimble; Candi Phillips; Debbie Engel; Connie Ashbrook; Henry Hood; and Russ Padden.

I would like to thank the staff at the Multnomah County and Lake Oswego Libraries. They were always courteous and I have a great appreciation of interlibrary loans.

I am grateful to Lolita Burnette for providing editorial assistance, to Gail Nelson for taking my draft and putting it into a camera ready copy, and to Sacha Barkhuff for photo editing and taking my vague ideas and creating the cover.

If you have parents, grandparents, friends, or relatives that either served in the military in World War II or on the Home Front, you may want to go to www.wwiimemorial.com and register the individual(s) in the Registry of Remembrances.

If you recognize in this book a long lost coworker or shipmate, you may contact me c/o Thomas/Wright, Inc., 7190 SW Fir Loop, Tigard, OR 97223. I will pass your contact information on to the person you recognize.

Notes

Chapter One - The Jurjevic Sisters

1. Vera Drab, Ann Thomas, and Jul Kurtek, interview with author, October 14, 2001.
2. *Dictionary of American Naval Fighting Ships, Volume VIII*; James H. Moody, Editor, (Washington, D.C.: Naval Historical Center, Department of the Navy, 1981), p. 570.
3. Churchill, Winston S., *Their Finest Hour*, (Boston: Houghton Mifflin Company, 1949), p. 252.
4. Vera Drab, interview with author, October 14, 2001.
5. Lloyd Pace, letter to author, March 5, 2003.
6. Vera Drab, interview with author, October 14, 2001.
7. Ibid.
8. Ibid.
9. *Dravo Slant*, Newspaper for Dravo war-workers. November 6, 1944, p.2.
10. Vera Drab, interview with author, October 14, 2001.
11. Trimble, William F., "Pittsburgh's Dravo Corporation and Naval Shipbuilding in World War II", *The American Neptune*, A Quarterly Journal of Maritime History, (Salem, Massachusetts: The Peabody Museum of Salem, October 1978), p. 275-276.
12. *A Story of Uncommon Enterprise, The Story of Dravo Corporation 1891-1966*, (Pittsburgh, Pennsylvania: Dravo Corporation), p. 69.
13. Trimble, p. 277.
14. Ann Thomas, and Jul Kurtek, interview with author, October 14, 2001.
15. Churchill, Winston S., *Their Finest Hour*, p. 101.
16. Ibid., p. 251.
17. McGee, William L., *The Amphibians Are Coming! Emergence of the 'Gator Navy and its Revolutionary Landing Craft*, (Santa Barbara, California: BMC Publications, 2000), p. 120-121.
18. Ann Thomas, interview with author, October 14, 2001.
19. Ibid.
20. Frank Thomas, letter to author, September 2003.
21. Frank M. Thomas Life Story, unpublished.
22. Ann Thomas, interview with author, September 26, 2003.
23. Frank Thomas, letter to author, September 2003.
24. Frank M. Thomas Life Story, unpublished.

25. Frank Thomas, letter to Ann Jurjevic, August 7, 1942.
26. Frank M. Thomas Life Story, unpublished.
27. Frank Thomas, letter to Ann Jurjevic, August 11, 1942.
28. Ibid.
29. Frank M. Thomas Life Story, unpublished.
30. Ibid.
31. Ibid.
32. www.inside1st.com, *An Inside Look: Landing Ship Tank, Dravo*.
33. Ibid.
34. Jul Kurtek, interview with author, October 14, 2001.
35. Ibid.
36. Ibid.
37. Trimble, William F., p. 281.
38. Jul Kurtek, interview with author, October 14, 2001.
39. Vera Drab, interview with author, October 14, 2001.
40. Ann Shearer, letter to author, February 2003.
41. Lester Parker, letter to author, March 2002.

Chapter Two - Just Another Day in the Shipyard

1. *Dravo Slant*, Newspaper for Dravo war workers. February 26, 1943. p. 3.
2. Ibid.
3. Johanna Aul, phone conversation with author, January 2, 2004.
4. Churchill, Winston S., *Closing the Ring*, (Boston, Massachusetts: Houghton Mifflin Company, 1951), p. 253-254.
5. Marie Talpas, phone conversation with author, February 9, 2004.
6. Ibid.
7. Ibid.
8. Churchill, p. 514.
9. Ann Toia, phone conversation with author, March 22, 2004.
10. Ibid.
11. Ibid.
12. Edward Neubauer, phone conversation with author, March 22, 2004.
13. Ibid.
14. Ibid.
15. Minnie Landry, phone conversation with author, March 22, 2004.
16. Ibid.
17. Ibid.
18. Ibid.
19. *A Story of Uncommon Enterprise, The Story of Dravo Corporation 1891 - 1966*, (Pittsburgh, Pennsylvania: Dravo Corporation), p. 76-78.

20. Cliff Kincaid, letters to author, February 5, 2003 and March 7, 2003 and Keays, Alan J., "His Ship was Blown Out of the Water," Dover, New Hampshire, *Daily Democrat* newspaper, June 6, 1994.
21. Cliff Kincaid, letter to author, February 5, 2003.
22. Dorothy Pecora, letters to author, February 22, 2003 and March 6, 2003.
23. Dorothy Pecora, letter to author, March 6, 2003.
24. Dorothy Pecora, letters to author, February 22, 2003 and March 6, 2003.

Chapter Three - Large Slow Targets

1. Juanita Wise Santos, letter to author, October 21, 2003.
2. Ibid.
3. Ibid.
4. Ibid.
5. Clark, Andrew L., *A Cornfield Shipyard*, (Mt. Vernon, Indiana: Windmill Publications, Inc., 1991), p. 59.
6. Hoyt, Edwin P., *The Invasion Before Normandy, The Secret Battle of Slapton Sands*, (New York: Stein and Day, 1985), p. 100.
7. MacDonald, Charles, R., "Slapton Sands: The Cover-up That Never Was," *Army 38*, No.6, June 1988, p. 64-67.
8. Hoyt, p. 103.
9. Clark, p. 59.
10. Hoyt, p. 103.
11. Clark, p. 60.
12. Adelbert Sickley, phone conversation with author, February 6, 2004.
13. Ibid.
14. Ibid.
15. Earl Minard, phone conversation with author, February 13, 2004.
16. Ibid.
17. BSAC Travel Club website, www.bsactravelclub.co.uk.
18. Hoyt, p. 114.
19. Lewis, Nigel, *Exercise Tiger, The Dramatic True Story of a Hidden Tragedy of World War II,* (New York: Prentice Hall Press, 1990), p. 104-105.
20. Hoyt, p. 134.
21. Hoyt, p. 115.
22. Clark, p. 60.
23. Lewis, p. 117.
24. MacDonald, p. 64-67.
25. Pecora, David V., *Between the Raindrops*, (New York: The Vantage Press, 1998), p. 97-98.
26. Adelbert Sickley, phone conversation with author, February 6, 2004.

Chapter Four - The Navy Yards

1. Black, Frederick R., *Charlestown Navy Yard, 1890-1973*, (Boston, Massachusetts: U.S. Department of Interior, Cultural Resources Management Study No. 20, 1988), Volume II, p. 571.
2. Art Hamilton, sent to author in February 2003 article entitled *U.S.S. Meeker County, LST-980*, author unknown.
3. Ibid.
4. Adrian Albrecht, letter to author, February 2, 2003.
5. Peter J. Maurin, letter to author, February 2, 2004.
6. Roger Noreen, letter to author, February 2, 2003.
7. Ibid.
8. Pyle, Ernie, *Brave Men*, (New York: Henry Holt and Company, 1944), p. 228.
9. Ibid., p. 232.
10. William A. Johnson, letter to author, February 5, 2003.
11. Ibid.
12. Ibid.
13. Don Cubley, letter to author, March 3, 2003.
14. *Dictionary of American Naval Fighting Ships, Volume III*, James H. Moody, Editor, (Washington, D.C.: Naval Historical Center, Department of the Navy; 1981), p. 960.
15. www.lstmemorial.org, The USS LST Ship Memorial website including Captain Jornlin's Account of the Voyage.
16. Earle, Fred M., "Employment of Women in the Navy Yards," *U.S. Naval Institute Proceedings*, September 1945, Volume 71, p. 1057.

Chapter Five - Bring It Back

1. John Massey, Letter to author, March 10, 2003.
2. Virginia Wittman, phone conversation with author, March 16, 2004.
3. Ibid.
4. Ibid.
5. Ibid.
6. *U.S. Steel News*, "River Yard Builds Navy Ships," April 1944, p. 9.
7. Lois Leseman, letter to author, November 2003 and phone conversation with author, October 2003.
8. Lois Leseman, phone conversation with author, October 2003 and phone conversation with author, February 6, 2004.

9. *U.S. Steel News*, p. 9.
10. Lois Leseman, phone conversation with author, February 6, 2004.
11. Ibid.
12. Ibid.
13. Springle, Ray, "LST Crash-Lands in Ohio and Gives Guests 'Battle Thrill'", *Pittsburgh Post Gazette*, October 28, 1943.
14. York, Mr. and Mrs. Joseph C., "*The Story of the LST 282*", Boise, Idaho, 1946, from Tom Aubuts' LST 282 web page, www.landships.com/282.
15. "*Official "Secret" Report of Loss of Ship, USS LST 282"*, Fleet Post Office, New York, New York, File No. 44-1 Serial 005, September 2, 1944, from Tom Aubuts' LST 282 web page, www.landships.com/282
16. York, Mr. and Mrs. Joseph C., "*The Story of the LST 282*", Boise, Idaho, 1946, from Tom Aubuts' LST 282 web page, www.landships.com/282.
17. Bergner, Hans E., "*Taking the Fight to France*", text of article appeared in Naval History magazine, March/April 1994, from Tom Aubuts' LST 282 web page, www.landships.com/282.
18. Adams, Ralph C., *USS LST 286*, and *LST 286* ship's log.
19. Ibid.
20. Ibid.
21. Ibid.
22. Lois Leseman, phone conversation with author, February 6, 2004.
23. Lois Leseman, letter to author, November 2003 and phone conversation with author, February 6, 2004.
24. Ibid.
25. John Massey, letter to author, February 5, 2003.
26. Lois Leseman, letter to author, November 2003.

Chapter Six - We're Saving Your Country

1. Mary Fisher, letter to Ron Adams' writing class at Broadmeadows Middle School in Quincy, MA, December 2 1992.
2. Melvin Smith, letter to author, January 4, 2004.
3. Cutler, Thomas J., *The Battle of Leyte Gulf, 23-26 October 1944,* (New York: Harper Collins Publishers, 1994), p. 3-5.
4. Mary Fisher, letter to Ron Adams' writing class at Broadmeadows Middle School in Quincy, MA, December 2 1992.
5. Ibid.
6. Mary Fisher, phone conversation with author, April 23, 2003.
7. *"Remembering the Hingham Shipyard,"* video, (Hingham, MA: The Hingham Shipyard Historical Foundation, 2000).

8. Mary Fisher, letter to Ron Adams' writing class at Broadmeadows Middle School in Quincy, MA, December 2 1992.
9. Mary Fisher, letter to author, May 23, 2003.
10. Mary Fisher, letter to Ron Adams' writing class at Broadmeadows Middle School in Quincy, MA, December 2 1992.
11. Mary Fisher, phone conversation with author, April 23, 2003.
12. Mary Fisher, letter to Ron Adams' writing class at Broadmeadows Middle School in Quincy, MA, December 2 1992.
13. Ibid.
14. Ibid.
15. Mary Fisher, phone conversation with author, April 23, 2003.
16. Mary Fisher, letter to Ron Adams' writing class at Broadmeadows Middle School in Quincy, MA, December 2 1992.
17. *"Remembering the Hingham Shipyard,"* video, (Hingham, MA: The Hingham Shipyard Historical Foundation, 2000).
18. Mary Fisher, letter to Ron Adams' writing class at Broadmeadows Middle School in Quincy, MA, December 2 1992.
19. St. John, Lt. Joseph F. as told to Howard Handleman, *Leyte Calling...*, (New York: The Vanguard Press, Inc., 1945), p. 10-23.
20. Ibid. p 62-86.
21. Ibid. p. 126-130.
22. Ibid. p. 186.
23. Cutler, Thomas J., p. 78.
24. Ibid. p. 54-55.
25. Frances Catrabone, letter to author, June 2, 2003.
26. Ibid.
27. Ibid.
28. Ibid.
29. Cutler, Thomas J., p. xiii.
30. Ibid., p. 264.
31. Ibid. p. 265-266.
32. Ibid. p. 267.
33. Ibid. p. 267.
34. Kenneth York, phone conversation with author, January 21, 2004.
35. Ibid.
36. Ibid.
37. Ibid.
38. Ibid.
39. George Lewis, phone conversation with author, January 24, 2004.
40. George Lewis, article written for *"The Scuttlebutt,"* December 28, 1995.

41. Ibid.
42. Ibid.
43. Ibid.
44. Kenneth York, phone conversation with author, January 21, 2004.
45. Melvin Smith, letter to author, February 7, 2003.
46. Ibid.
47. Mary Fisher, phone conversation with author, April 23, 2003.

Chapter Seven - The Prairie Shipyard

1. Mabel L. Ward, phone conversation with author, March 15, 2004.
2. Ibid.
3. Ibid.
4. Ibid.
5. Ibid.
6. *Our Prairie Shipyard, Historical Edition, 1942-1945*, (Seneca, Illinois: Chicago Bridge & Iron Co., 1945), p. 23 and 42.
7. Laura J. Cox, phone conversation with author, March 15, 2004.
8. Ibid.
9. Ibid.
10. Ibid.
11. Ibid.
12. Alla E. Beard, letter to author, February 8, 2003.
13. Betty Mosher, phone conversation with author, April 30, 2004.
14. Ibid.
15. Ibid.
16. L. F. Grove, letter to Russ Kopplow, May 2, 1994.

Chapter Eight - Never Late for an Invasion

1. Hall, C. Ray, "Ship Saved by Veterans Honors Them," *The Courier Journal*, Louisville, Kentucky, July 25, 2003.
2. Ruie Golden, letter to author, August 7, 2003 and phone conversation with author, August 14, 2003.
3. Ruie Golden, phone conversation with author, August 14, 2003.
4. Ibid.
5. Clark, Andrew L., *A Cornfield Shipyard*, (Mt. Vernon, Indiana: Windmill Publications, Inc., 1991), p. 1.
6. Ibid. p.1.
7. Ruie Golden, letter to author, August 7, 2003.
8. Ruie Golden, phone conversation with author, August 14, 2003.

9. Ibid.
10. Ibid.
11. Ibid.
12. Ruie Golden, letter to author, August 7, 2003 and phone conversation with author, August 14, 2003.
13. Ruie Golden, phone conversation with author, August 14, 2003.
14. Ibid.
15. Ibid.
16. Ibid.
17. Ibid.
18. Ibid.
19. Lloyd Pace, letter to author, March 31, 2003.
20. Lloyd Pace, letter to author, May 17, 2003.
21. Lloyd Pace, letter to author, March 31, 2003.
22. Pauline Evans, phone conversation with author, February 3, 2004.
23. Ibid.
24. Ibid.
25. Ibid.
26. Ibid.
27. Ibid.
28. Ibid.
29. Johnson, William L.C., *The West Loch Story, Hawaii's Second Greatest Disaster in Terms of Casualties,* (Seattle, Washington: Westloch Publications, 1986), p. 11-20.
30. Ibid. p. 12-14.
31. Ibid. p. 14-20.
32. King Richeson, phone conversation with author, January 28, 2004.
33. King Richeson, copy of Navy Court of Inquiry, May 1944 and letter to individual researching for the History Channel Documentary "Explosions." March 14, 2001.
34. Ibid.
35. Carlyle Harmer, letter to author, February 2004.
36. Cooney, Lisa, "Kamikazees, typhoon aim at doughty LST seamen", *Pottsviille Republican & Herald,* January 25, 2002, schuylkill.com.
37. Tabin, Seymour, Memo, March 8, 2003.
38. Edith Jones, phone conversation with author, September 15, 2003.
39. Edith Jones, phone conversation with author, February 9, 2004.
40. Ibid.
41. Johnson, William L.C., p. 100.
42. Ibid. p. 130.

43. Ibid. p. 134.
44. Ibid. p. 141.
45. Ibid. p. 143.
46. Ibid. p. 143 -144.
47. Ibid. p. 149.
48. Ibid. p. 150.
49. Ibid. p. 105.
50. Carlyle Harmer, letter to author, February 2004.
51. Hoover, Bill, www.kilroywashere.org/007-Pages/07-Searches.html
52. Johnson, William L.C., p. 67.
53. Ibid. p. 67.
54. Francis Hillibush, email to author, February 11, 2004.
55. Johnson, William L.C., p. 15-21.
56. Catherine Allin, correspondence with author, December 2003.
57. Ibid.
58. Ibid.
59. Virginia Broxton, correspondence with author, August 2003.
60. Bryan, Linda, "Let Me Call You Sweetheart", *The Southeast Sun, Enterprise*, Alabama, February 14, 1996.
61. Ibid.
62. Ibid.
63. Ibid.
64. Ibid.
65. Ibid.
66. Ibid.
67. Virginia Broxton, correspondence with author, August 2003.
68. Ibid.
69. Augustine DeLong, phone conversation with author, March 2, 2004.
70. E.J. Goodfriend, letter to author, March 21, 2003.
71. E.J. Goodfriend, letter to author, February 8, 2003.

Chapter Nine - The Mystery Ship

1. Lane, Frederic C., *Ships for Victory, A History of Shipbuilding Under the U.S. Maritime Commission in World War II*, (Baltimore and London: The Johns Hopkins University Press, 1951 and 2001), p. 610 - 611.
2. *Bo's 'n's Whistle*, Volume 2, No. 18, September 27, 1942, p. 11.
3. *Bo's 'n's Whistle*, Volume 2 , No. 20, October 22, 1942, p. 4.
4. *Bo's 'n's Whistle*, Volume 2, No. 22, November 26, 1942, p. 2.
5. *Bo's 'n's Whistle*, Volume 3, No. 20, October 21, 1943, p. 2.

6. Alice Nenemay Camel, letter to author, February 12, 2004.
7. Ibid.
8. Carlyle Harmer, letter to author, February 2004.
9. Ibid.
10. Ibid.
11. Ibid.

Chapter Ten - Other Ships/Other Trades

1. Jean Hayes, letter to author, January 26, 2004.
2. Ibid.
3. Ibid.
4. Nell Conley, interview with author, March 29, 2003.
5. Ibid.
6. Ibid.
7. Ibid.
8. Madra Hullinger, letters to author, February 19, 2003 and August 2003.
9. Ibid.
10. Louise Phalen, letter to author, February 2003.
11. Mavis Kyle, letter to author, June 23, 2003.
12. Mavis Kyle, letters to author, June 23, 2003 and February 2003.
13. Mavis Kyle, letter to author, February 2003.
14. Dora Jockumsen, letter to author, May 2003.
15. Ibid.
16. Ibid.
17. Dorothy Kiggans, letter to author, March 1, 2003.
18. Ibid.
19. Ibid.
20. Ibid.
21. Ibid.
22. Ibid.

Chapter Eleven - State of Life

1. Blossom Ann Kocher, interview with author, October 5, 2002.
2. Ibid.
3. Ibid.
4. Ibid.
5. Ibid.
6. Ibid.

7. Ibid.
8. Ibid.
9. Ibid.

Chapter Twelve - The Korean War

1. Major Thomas, letter to author, February 2003.
2. Ibid.
3. Ibid.
4. Ibid.
5. Ibid.
6. Ibid.
7. Richard Arnold, letter to author, March 15, 2004.
8. *Dictionary of American Naval Fighting Ships*, James H. Moody, Editor (Washington, D.C.: Naval Historical Center, Department of the Navy, 1981), Volume VII, p. 570-571.
9. Russ Kopplow, letter to author, February 5, 2003.
10. Ibid.
11. Ibid.
12. Russ Kopplow, letter to author, March 8, 2004.
13. Ibid.
14. Russ Kopplow, letter to author, February 5, 2003.

Bibliography

"Achievement in Many Related Fields," *Bulletin 901,* Pittsburgh, Pennsylvania: Dravo Corporation, 1946.

A Story of Uncommon Enterprise, The Story of Dravo Corporation 1891 - 1966, Pittsburgh, Pennsylvania: Dravo Corporation.

Adams, Ralph C., *USS LST 286,* and *LST 286* ship's log.

Barbey, Daniel E., *MacArthur's Amphibious Navy,* Annapolis, Maryland: Naval Institute Press, 1971.

Bergner, Hans E., "*Taking the Fight to France*", text of article appeared in Naval History magazine, March/April 1994, from Tom Aubuts' LST 282 web page, www.landships.com/282.

Berner, Thomas F., *The Brooklyn Navy Yard,* Charleston, South Carolina: Arcadia Publishing, 1999.

Bither, Barbara A., *Charlestown Navy Yard,* Charleston, South Carolina: Arcadia Publishing, 1999.

Black, Frederick R., *Charlestown Navy Yard, 1890-1973,* Boston, Massachusetts: U.S. Department of Interior, Cultural Resources Management Study No. 20, 1988, Volume II.

Bo's 'n's Whistle, Volume 2, No. 18, September 27, 1942.

Bo's 'n's Whistle, Volume 2 , No. 20, October 22, 1942, p. 4.

Bo's 'n's Whistle, Volume 2, No. 22, November 26, 1942, p. 2.

Bo's 'n's Whistle, Volume 3, No. 20, October 21, 1943, p. 2.

Bryan, Linda, "Let Me Call You Sweetheart", *The Southeast Sun, Enterprise,* Alabama, February 14, 1996.

Churchill, Winston S., *Closing the Ring,* Boston, Massachusetts: Houghton Mifflin Company, 1951.

Churchill, Winston S., *Their Finest Hour,* Boston: Houghton Mifflin Company, 1949.

Clark, Andrew L., *A Cornfield Shipyard,* Mt. Vernon, Indiana: Windmill Publications, Inc., 1991.

Cooney, Lisa, "Kamikazees, typhoon aim at doughty LST seamen", *Pottsville Republican & Herald,* January 25, 2002, schuylkill.com.

Cressman, Robert J., *The Official Chronology of the U.S. Navy in World War II,* Annapolis, Maryland: Naval Institute Press, 2000.

Cutler, Thomas J., *The Battle of Leyte Gulf, 23-26 October 1944,* New York: Harper Collins Publishers, 1994.

Dorwart, Jeffery M. with Wolf, Jean K., *The Philadelphia Navy Yard*, Philadelphia, Pennsylvania: University of Pennsylvania Press, 2001.

Dravo Slant, Newspaper for Dravo war workers. February 26, 1943.

Dravo Slant, Newspaper for Dravo war-workers. November 6, 1944.

Earle, Fred M., "Employment of Women in the Navy Yards," *U.S. Naval Institute Proceedings*, September 1945, Volume 71.

Fore N' Aft, October 15, 1942; October 29, 1942; and April 23, 1943.

Good Work Sister! Women Shipyard Workers of World War II, An Oral History, video, Portland, Oregon: Northwest Women's History Project, 1982.

Gourley, Harold E., *Shipyard Work Force, World's Champion LST Builders on the Beautiful Ohio, 1942-1945, Evansville, IN*, Mt. Vernon, Indiana: Windmill Publications, Inc., 1996.

Hall, C. Ray, "Ship Saved by Veterans Honors Them", *The Courier Journal*, Louisville, Kentucky, July 25, 2003.

Hoyt, Edwin P., *The Invasion Before Normandy, The Secret Battle of Slapton Sands*, New York: Stein and Day, 1985.

Johnson, William L.C., *The West Loch Story, Hawaii's Second Greatest Disaster in Terms of Casualties,* Seattle, Washington: Westloch Publications, 1986.

Kaiser Co., Inc., *Vessels Construction Program Report for Period Ending January 31st, 1943,* Contract Mcc 7467.

Keays, Alan J., "His Ship was Blown Out of the Water," Dover, New Hampshire, *Daily Democrat* newspaper, June 6, 1994.

Kellar, Patricia C. and James H., *Evansville Shipyard, Outside Any Shipbuilding Zone,* Bloomington, Indiana: Round Hill Press, 1999.

Kershaw, Alex, *The Bedford Boys*, Cambridge, Massachusetts: Da Capo Press, 2003.

Kesselman, Amy Vita, *Fleeting Opportunities: Women Shipyard Workers in Portland and Vancouver during World War II and Reconversion*, Albany, New York: University of New York Press, 1990.

Knox, James W., *The Birth of the LST*, Georgetown, Pennsylvania: The Pennsylvania LST Association, 2000.

Ladd, J.D., *Assault From The Sea 1939-45, The Craft, The Landings, The Men*, New York: Hippocrene Books, Inc., 1976.

Lane, Frederic C., *Ships for Victory, A History of Shipbuilding Under the U.S. Maritime Commission in World War II,* Baltimore and London: The Johns Hopkins University Press, 1951 and 2001.

Lewis, Nigel, *Exercise Tiger, The Dramatic True Story of a Hidden Tragedy of World War II,* New York: Prentice Hall Press, 1990.

MacDonald, Charles, R., "Slapton Sands: The Cover-up That Never Was," *Army 38*, No.6, June 1988.

McGee, William L., *The Amphibians Are Coming! Emergence of the 'Gator Navy and its Revolutionary Landing Craft*, Santa Barbara, California: BMC Publications, 2000.

Moody, James H., Editor, *Dictionary of American Naval Fighting Ships*, Washington, D.C.: Naval Historical Center, Department of the Navy, 1981, Volumes III, VII, and VII.

O'Donnell, Victoria and Monaco, Paul, *Women, War, and Work; Shaping Space for Productivity in the Shipyard during the Second World War*, video, Bozeman, Montana: KUSN-TV Montana Public Television, 1997.

"*Official "Secret" Report of Loss of Ship, USS LST 282"*, Fleet Post Office, New York, New York, File No. 44-1 Serial 005, September 2, 1944, from Tom Aubuts' LST 282 web page, www.landships.com/282.

Our Prairie Shipyard, Historical Edition, 1942-1945, Seneca, Illinois: Chicago Bridge & Iron Co., 1945.

Pecora, David V., *Between the Raindrops*, New York: The Vantage Press, 1998.

Polmar, Norman and Allen, Thomas B., *World War II, America at War, 1941-1945*, New York: Random House, Inc., 1991.

Pyle, Ernie, *Brave Men*, New York: Henry Holt and Company, 1944.

Remembering the Hingham Shipyard, video, Hingham, MA: The Hingham Shipyard Historical Foundation, 2000.

Roosevelt, Eleanor and MacGregor, Frances Cook, *This is America*, New York: G.P. Putnam's Sons, 1942.

St. John, Lt. Joseph F. as told to Howard Handleman, *Leyte Calling...*, New York: The Vanguard Press, Inc., 1945.

Springle, Ray, "LST Crash-Lands in Ohio and Gives Guests 'Battle Thrill'", *Pittsburgh Post Gazette*, October 28, 1943.

Trimble, William F., "Pittsburgh's Dravo Corporation and Naval Shipbuilding in World War II", *The American Neptune*, A Quarterly Journal of Maritime History, Salem, Massachusetts: The Peabody Museum of Salem, October 1978.

U.S. Steel News, "River Yard Builds Navy Ships," April 1944.

York, Mr. and Mrs. Joseph C., "*The Story of the LST 282*", Boise, Idaho, 1946, from Tom Aubuts' LST 282 web page, www.landships.com/282.

Websites

www.abiz4me.com/lst.html

www.beadee.com/kaiser/index.shtml

www.bsactravelclub.com

www.coltoncompany.com/shipbuilding/usshipbldrs.htm

www.courier-journal.com

www.history.navy.mil/

www.ibiblio.org/hyperwar/

www.insidelst.com

www.kilroywashere.org

www.landships.com/282/

www.lstmemorial.org

www.navsource.org

www.schuylkill.com

www.wwiimemorial.com